I MARRIED A BLANKET THIEF

Surviving and Thriving in Married Life

LONNY CAREY

malcolm down

PUBLISHING

This book is dedicated to my soulmate and best friend, Sara. What adventures we have had in thirty-nine years of marriage. I wouldn't trade a single day.
I love you dearly.

There are many virtuous and capable women in the world, but you surpass them all!
Proverbs 31:29 NLT

Author Note:

I have written this book as a work of creative nonfiction. The events are portrayed to the best of my memory. They reflect my present recollection of experiences over time. While all the stories in this book are true, some names and identifying details have been changed to protect the privacy of the people involved.

Contents

Foreword

Never before has there been a greater need for books that herald the wonder and power of marriage between one man and one woman.

My friend Lonny Carey has written a brilliant and insightful tale of how real relationships work out on the ground, with all their up and downs, twists and turns and highs and lows. It is also ultimately a tale of Jesus and his Church.

Marriage is a picture of a far greater, cosmic and spiritual reality and in the pages of this book you will catch glimpses of the glory of God revealed in the lives of two ordinary people, serving an extraordinary God together. You will laugh, cry, gasp, smile and maybe even shed the occasional tear as you read Lonny's honest and funny story of his and Sara's friendship through the years.

I wholeheartedly recommend this book – it will do you good!

Phil Wilthew
Author of *Developing Prophetic Culture: Building healthy churches that hear Jesus clearly* (Malcolm Down Publishing, 2016)

Let's Get Introduced

If you think women are the weaker sex, try pulling the blankets back to your side.

This year, Sara and I have been married thirty-nine years. So, what have I learned in that time; what is the key to a good marriage?

For starters, I have learned to tuck in my side of the bed. I have also learned that when the big Men-O starts, blankets are both optional and compulsory within minutes of each other. It's blankets on, blankets off.

Why is it that men get the blame for the menopause? It's in the name, I know, but we are the ones who are put on pause with the same off and on approach. 'Don't cuddle me. I am too hot! why aren't you cuddling me? I am freezing!'

I have also learned that flannelette sheets are the bane of a man's life. Combined with that most evil of all clothing, hard to access, impossible to remove flannelette pyjamas, my wife sticks to the sheets like two sides of Velcro. Together, this ensures there is little in the way of movement, which is great for stopping the blanket stealing but makes for a lonely night.

What else? Well, I know that going to sleep at night cuddling up to my wife is the nicest thing ever invented. Waking up to Sara is always a delight, especially when I see that she has done most of the blanket thievery and I can tease her about it.

This book is a light-hearted but serious look at marriage. I have no doubt that I married a blanket thief – my best catch ever.

Chapter One
Love at First Crunch

World Events

- 20th Century Fox is heavily promoting the film, The *Other Side of Midnight*, thinking *Star Wars* would be a flop
- Elvis Presley dies, aged forty-two
- I, Lonny, turn nineteen at El Rancho Children's Camp

I am now in my sixties. If you ask me if I believe in love at first sight, I would without hesitation have scoffed at such Hollywood nonsense. And yet…

My blanket-stealing wife stole my heart when she was just seventeen years old, at a Children's Christian Camp in New Zealand where we were both leaders.

She walked into the great hall with her friend and together they surveyed the talent around the room. Unbeknown to me, I was the top prize. Both of them joked that I would be their boyfriend one day. And so, Sara hatched a plot, not consciously, but deep in the swirling chaos of what we call attraction.

I, on the other hand, am less complicated and fell for her immediately. Being a bloke and of a serious nature, I just couldn't keep my eyes off her tight patchy jeans. Sara wooed me with her other talents too. She was very confident but friendly and every day she read a chapter from a book to the entire camp. You could have heard a pin drop when she was reading and I'm sure my jaw was permanently dropped and my heart rate elevated.

The funny thing was that, despite the joking, neither of us wanted a relationship at that time. Sara was about to go to the USA for a year on a Rotary Exchange[1] and did not want the entanglement that came with a boyfriend. I was still grieving over a broken heart and was determined to stay pure in the faith – without girls in my life.

So here we were, the long-haired, bearded, vegetarian hippie in his kaftan (aka the Old Testament Prophet) and Sara, in her tight patchy jeans and bubbly personality, both trying to remain aloof and in control.

The whole camp was aware of our predicament and the budding romance – except us. And it seemed that the Lord continually threw us together. By chance, if you believe in that, we were in the same team. We developed chants together and fought the good fight to ensure our team won the most points.

The two of us led our cohort in the commando course. Sara was covered in mud and sweat and I was hauling kids over the climbing wall. I had to reach down and grab her by the shorts and pull her over. That adrenaline was all we needed to win the race.

During the night, her young girls would sneak out of their cabin and meet up with my boys. Sara thought it harmless fun. My boys took advantage of their physically exhausted leader, in a half-sleep state distractedly thinking about the mud-covered girl of his dreams. They would ask, one at a time, to go to the toilet until I finally realised I was the only one left in the cabin. I would then march out the door and shoo them back to their beds amidst many giggles and complaints.

I fell in love that week with my wife-to-be.

A few weeks before the camp, a friend had been urging me to attend as they were short on leaders. Having been once before, I knew it was a spiritual buzz and I needed some of that. I was battling with rejection over my last relationship and all the horrible things that had happened. I was struggling with my faith and becoming desperate for a breakthrough, to have something positive happen in what had been, so far, a very bleak year.

So, I plucked up courage and went to see my boss at the plastics factory where I worked as a lab technician. He was difficult to approach. To make matters worse we were very busy at that time and I, being new, had accrued no annual leave.

To my utter surprise and delight he told me that the factory closed down for maintenance each year during that very week. When it comes to the 'chance' or 'ordained' argument, I will go for the purposeful plan architected by a loving God.

Finally, on my nineteenth birthday, at the end of that week, I found the backbone to ask Sara if I could talk with her. I bought a pottle of crunchy nut yogurt and asked if she would come for a walk with me. Apparently, she was terrified that I was going to tell her off about the girls sneaking out of her cabin. She had no idea that I was interested in her.

As we walked down the treelined lane of El Rancho, I asked if I could get to know her better by visiting her in Wellington. I lived 140 kilometres away in another city and had no car – but to a teenager in love this was just a minor detail.

Asking her to take that walk was probably the hardest thing I had ever done. Being a coward by nature, as all men are until they discover the hero inside, I had already tried to get her phone number from her little brother, Simon. His cheeky reply to me was, 'Ask her yourself.' It is fortunate that I took his advice.

Sara said yes to getting to know me and the deal was sealed by the crunchy nut yogurt. That is when I knew I had fallen for her, it was love at first crunch.

Is infatuation good, does it last, is it love? The answer is a little bit of yes and lot of no. Fascination and even fixation with each other is a start which can lead to a something deeper and more lasting.

On the other hand, Hollywood insists that love is a state of longing, where the lovers have constant butterflies in their tummies and skip through each day all light-headed and irrational. It paints an ugly picture of passionate love being reserved only for the young and the beautiful.

Infatuation depends on self-serving emotions and has a short lifespan. It usually dies after a few months but can struggle on for several years. Real love replaces it. This love is a deliberate choice we make each day despite our feelings. We decide not to fall out of love but to devote our lives to one another, regardless.

At this point I can say that we were obsessed with each other but this obsession started a relationship that has spanned forty years, where she continues to steal my heart and my blankets on a daily basis.

Message to men (MTM)

Infatuation has a role to play when it comes to love. But be wary of its dangers once you are in a relationship.

None of us will go through life without being attracted to other people. We are all uniquely wired. And so, certain people press all the right buttons for us – they catch our eye and bombard the brain with a rush of desire. It's not wrong, it's completely natural.

However, our over-fertile minds can feed this attraction until it becomes pure infatuation. The soil of loneliness, disappointment, frustration and anger at your spouse can grow into an unhealthy obsession with another that will eventually poison your relationship.

Deal with it! Infatuation can be a step towards learning to love someone but it is far from the genuine thing. It will not endure, but giving into it outside of marriage will have disastrous consequences that last a lifetime. Don't be that guy, be wise and have the tenacity to put right whatever is coming between you and the love of your life.

But the man who commits adultery is an utter fool, for he destroys himself. He will be wounded and disgraced. His shame will never be erased.
Proverbs 6:32-33, NLT

Chapter Two
Fight the Good Fight

World Events
- The 'High Five' is created by two Los Angeles Dodgers
- 'God Defend New Zealand' became that country's national anthem
- Gold is just $161 USD per ounce
- I buy a hotted-up car to visit Sara

Here we were, two teenagers separated by distance with only phone calls and letters to connect our hearts and minds.

Well, actually, it was only letters, as our phone calls tend to be a bit brisk and a little awkward. We both grew up in households that discouraged the use of the telephone, especially expensive toll-calls. As such, Sara and I seemed to have mutated into phone trolls who were not that friendly when forced to make conversation into the telling-bone. And we are still that way, four decades later.

So, letters it was, which in the end proved to be my most valuable arsenal for winning the heart of my beloved. But for the next four months, before Sara began her sojourn to the United States of America, we visited each other whenever we could.

I busted my gut at the plastics factory to earn enough money to buy a 'hotted-up' Mark II Ford Cortina. At that stage I didn't know my wife-to-be was a bit of a petrol-head and to my delight she was impressed by the noisy exhaust pipe and grunty engine.

These visits in the late 1970s were not always as romantic as you might imagine. I would fill the seemingly endless one-and-a-half-hour drive with images of us running into each other's arms, joyful that we were finally together again. This is not what happened. We wasted visit after visit fighting.

That's right – fighting. How we stayed together is as much of a miracle as how we got together in the first place. On my first trip, I picked up a couple of hitchhikers so I could share the gospel with them. It went really well and we talked heart-to-heart all the way to Wellington. I then dropped them off somewhere unknown to me, which meant I had to find my way back to the directions Sara had given me.

When I did find her street, the numbers suddenly ended when it came to a T-junction. I drove up and down in desperation and then finally gave away part of my manhood by asking for directions. This too turned out to be disastrous.

More time went by until I finally found the second half of the street. The two parts did not even join. It was then up a steep and windy road with limited letterbox numbering.

'Wow, the streets in Wellington are crazy,' I remember thinking. I parked my Cortina half-dangling on the side of a cliff and tentatively knocked on the door.

Sara's mum, Lesley, whom I had never met before, answered with, 'You're late and Sara has been very worried about you.' Not a good start, I thought, but things soon got worse. Sara appeared and took me into the kitchen for a drink. While we were happily chatting away this enormous voice boomed down from the sky saying, 'Don't mind her, she's bloody rude.'

It was her dad, known to all as Pop. He was up a ladder doing some handyman job and we hadn't seen him.

This visit was quickly going from bad to worse. It was dinnertime, so we all ate at the table, again with Sara and me chatting excitedly. We may have been bad at telephone conversations but we quickly came to realise that we both loved to talk face-to-face.

So here we were, merrily talking about mutual friends and reminiscing over the fateful camp where we met, when that booming voice cut in again, this time accompanied by a thump on the table, 'Quiet, it's the news!'

My heart sank. I seemed to have made a bad first impression on Sara's family. In fact, it took almost a decade to turn Pop's dislike for me around.

Sara and I then went for a drive to chat in peace. You might be thinking we went to some lovers' lane to make out but you would be wrong. In fact, I never held her hand for two months, as I was determined to be pure in our relationship and not to fall back into my wild non-Christian ways. Needless to say, coming from a huggy, demonstrative family, this frustrated Sara and made her feel like I was distant from her.

I don't recall us fighting that first time, but it soon became a pattern that lasted well into the first five years of our marriage. I was very black and white and quite intense as a young person. Hence, my nickname of 'Old Testament Prophet'.

However, many of my views were based on misinformation. As an example, I was opposed to the movement of the Holy Spirit, believing like most people at that time that it was solely given to kick-start the early Church and that it petered out when Peter petered out.

I had had some bad experiences when I was a young Christian in a new city looking for a church. Having grown up in a completely unchurched household I knew nothing about Christianity. It was all new to me and very puzzling. During my first visit to a church we sang the song 'Amazing Grace'. I remember saying to my friends afterwards, 'I have heard about Jesus and Mary but who is this Grace person?'

As a hippie and being very ignorant of churches, I had tried any building with a steeple. Needless to say, the conservative churches didn't know what to do with me and I did not feel in the least bit welcome. At the other extreme, I went to a church where they all spoke in tongues[2] at the same time. When the lady sitting next to me noticed that I didn't join in she scolded me, saying that it wasn't possible to be a Christian unless I spoke in tongues.

I was hurt and confused and decided just to read my Bible by myself and not to attend any church. I devoured the Word of God on my own for a year until I finally met some young Christian people who took me under their wing.

Sara on the other hand was Spirit-filled and dead keen to gently show me that there was more to Christianity. I was oblivious of the fact that she was deliberately taking me to meetings where the preacher spoke on the Holy Spirit. I argued; sometimes with her, sometimes with the preacher and not always in private.

As you can clearly see, we had major theological differences of opinion. But added to this, Sara was a leader among her peers; quick-minded, articulate and confident. I was more withdrawn, very analytical and entrenched in overly deep thinking. In fact, just last year, I found our love letters and proceeded to read one I'd written to her while she was in living in Ohio. I couldn't finish it – it was so heavy it exhausted me.

I too was a leader among my peers and so a power struggle began. We both dug our toes in over almost any issue and would end up in a huff.

I had very mixed thoughts during my one-and-a-half-hour drive back home after each visit – most of them not very nice. But I soon got over it and would miss her like crazy in the weeks between.

The big lesson which we took seven years to learn was to choose our battles and to give each other the benefit of the doubt.

Many of our fights resulted from the way we reacted to each other. Most of the time we misinterpreted each other as being bossy when no such thing was intended.

A quicker thinker than me, Sara often suggested something before I had had time to process and I resented that. I reacted badly and so did she.

Sara came from a close family where she tended to see her father's explosive behaviour as normal. She was prone to mimicking it without realising what it did to my fragile ego.

By choosing to think the best of each other and taking a deep breath, the power struggles eventually ceased. We learned to argue well, not to score points but to do our utmost to stick to the issue and to really listen.

I am happy to say that back then we argued a lot but these days it is very rare. We seem to have moved on to long discussions that are more constructive; many things simply cannot be resolved overnight or through one exhausting and brutal session.

Arguments like those we endured during the late 1970s and early 1980s were key to learning to trust each other. We needed to discover that in some areas it was OK to let the other one lead without feeling threatened. As natural leaders, it was important to work out where one was better at taking the lead and to allow them to do so with good grace and support. Real love is about having a servant heart towards each other. When this is combined with respect, it brings freedom and fosters love rather than creating an atmosphere of competition and misery.

Fighting the good fight is essential to working out who you are as a single entity. Not arguing can equally be very destructive and force you to silently feud in your own corner. A few years ago, we went on a ski trip to Canada. On this trip was a couple in their seventies whom we befriended. The husband very proudly told us that in forty years of marriage they had never had an argument. When he went off to get drinks, his wife confessed that she wished they did. She said there were many unspoken things that festered in their marriage and that refusing to bring them out into the open sometimes made her miserable.

So, fight if you must, hopefully not as much as we did, but fight the good fight in love.

Message to men (MTM)

Arguments too often become a competition. Our inherently aggressive nature as men means that we fight to win. We can become experts in shouting down and bullying our partners or overwhelming them with male logic until we feel like victors. But that sort of victory comes with a price.

Arguments that border on war have no winners. Disagreements are a natural and essential way of addressing differences together. How you resolve these is absolutely critical to how strong or weak your relationship will become.

Wake up! You are on the same side, the same team. Stop trying to win and start loving and respecting your wife – the avoidance of collateral damage and the strengthening of your marriage is of far more value than stroking your male ego.

Take time to think about how you argue. If you are aggressive and adversarial then it may surprise you to know that quarrels are seen by your wife as acts of hate, not love.

Turn those macho male traits into cherishing and protecting your marriage by learning to disagree in a healthy and mature way.

Hatred stirs up quarrels, but love makes up for all offenses.
Proverbs 10:12, NLT

Chapter Three
Taking a Dive

World Events

- *Jesus Christ* Superstar, the musical, opens in NYC
- France, USA and USSR all perform nuclear testing
- In New Zealand petrol is four times more expensive than 1973 following the oil crisis
- Sara and I attend her Seventh Form Ball

It's amazing how something supposed to be the most fun in your life can also be the most stressful. It was the time of year for the Seventh Form Ball and Sara wanted me to take her.

I felt like I had been asked to take a bungee dive without a cord. Everything about it had that falling sensation we have in dreams when you don't know how it will end. This turned out to be a classic nightmare.

The previous year, Sara's boyfriend at the time took her to the Sixth Form ball. He was extremely good-looking and very popular with everyone. He could dance, he could sing, he could play every musical instrument and any song by ear. On the night of the ball he turned up on his motorbike in a beautiful three-piece suit and swept Sara off her feet. Unfortunately for Sara, and very fortunately for me, he was in love with someone else who was overseas.

In stark contrast, I only owned kaftans and did not have a proper pair of shoes. Was I good-looking? Well, people often said that I looked like Jesus or Mick Fleetwood. Does that count? As far as bikes went, I had an old pushbike which had nearly killed me. I thought I could dance but couldn't. In my early days of being a Christian, people used to move away from me during the worship because I was so tuneless.

But I was resourceful, so I borrowed some shoes (which were too small) and a brown corduroy jacket with a tie. I drove to Wellington so nervous I had a case of the collywobbles. When the time came, I got into my fine attire at Sara's house and Lesley commented that I looked great which gave me a level of confidence I never should have had.

As the evening wore on my ill-fitting clothes came off. First the shoes, which were killing me. Next the scratchy jacket. I didn't want to lose the borrowed tie so I wrapped it around my head. At last I was free to dance with no inhibitions. And I did. The urban legend is that I topped things off by boogying down with my tongue hanging out. But I deny that.

The night was young so I was surprised when Sara developed a massive headache and had to be taken home.

The next day was uneventful and little was said between us, which was unusual. I did not know Sara had been up for most of night wrestling with whether to dump me before I completely ruined her reputation and her life. The moral of the story was: never invite a hippie to a formal ball. It will only end in tears or headaches.

That day we came very close to ending our relationship. There was no solid reason for Sara to continue going out with me. She wanted freedom to be young without ties while she was in the States. I had proved beyond doubt that I could be a major embarrassment. We fought a lot. Our views on key things like the Holy Spirit were not aligned. Everything about our backgrounds screamed at us that it would never work. And it very nearly didn't.

Yet somehow God kept intervening to keep us together. He had a plan for Sara and me that involved us staying together. Despite the hurdles that were to come, the Lord always found a way forward for us.

We survived the agony of that night without taking a dive and Sara didn't tell me she'd nearly dumped me until many years into our marriage.

Message to men (MTM)

How honest do you need to be for a relationship to work? We all have secrets, right? Honesty has to do with vulnerability and courage. These are key elements of a strong marriage which must start with being honest with yourself.

People constantly fool themselves into believing they are better than they are. One Australian study found 86 per cent of workers said their performance was above average. US researchers discovered that 80 per cent of people rated their driving as better than average. In one university survey, 25 per cent of students thought their leadership abilities ranked in the top 1 per cent.[3]

So much for the statistical bell curve.[4] Someone is fooling themselves and its most likely to be you and me. Honesty is painful and hard to achieve consistently, but in the end this is what will make us great men of God.

I am not referring here to being blunt and uncaring but combining truth with gentleness that considers others. Jesus is our supreme example in this as his life was all about truth, love and faith.

Honesty is the hub by which the spokes of authenticity, integrity, trust, honour, virtue and truth revolve. What woman wouldn't want that in a man, especially if he has the wisdom to combine honesty with kindness?

An honest answer is like a kiss on the lips.
Proverbs 24:26

Chapter Four
Ready or Not?

World Events

- Airbags in cars are promoted by some USA manufacturers as an alternative to wearing seat belts
- Average house price in New Zealand is $24,005
- New Zealand only has two television channels – colour TVs have been around for only three years
- I tell Sara I love her

At what stage can you both openly say you love each other? If one is in love and the other is not, a dangerous imbalance begins to tip your relationship. This common dilemma can scare off the not-yet-ready one. Equally, it can make the lovesick one look needy. This happened to Sara and me and should have spelt doom for us as a couple. But God had other plans.

Before we get to that tricky time, let me back up a bit. Despite living in different cities, we didn't spend all our time waiting for Facebook or Twitter to be invented. In fact, in 1977 we still had fourteen years to wait until the World Wide Web became publicly available.

We wrote letters and did our best to see each other despite the lack of screens and technology.

Once, Sara's parents shocked us both by agreeing that she could come to Palmerston North and stay at my flat. That time is painted in vivid colours on the inside of my mind. I had just splashed out and bought the Fleetwood Mac *Rumours* LP and since the two-month stand-down of not touching was over, we sat cuddled in the dark on our lounge floor listening to it over and over.

I still think it's the best album ever produced and want the song 'You Make Loving Fun'[5] to be played at my funeral. It so reminds me of those times and of the special girl who stole my heart before she stole my blankets.

Much later, when we had the fun of being parents to our three teenagers, we reflected back on those days. We wanted our children to avoid unnecessary temptation with their girlfriends and boyfriends.

There were several simple rules. If you are in the bedroom with them, the door must remain fully open. There was to be no snuggling down under the same blanket. Touching was confined to cuddles and kisses and nothing more than you would feel comfortable doing in front of your grandma. Our wonderful children respected these rules and saw the common sense behind them.

In our experience, there was no accountability for young Christians going out together. On reflection, this was so wrong, if not dangerous. Sara had a brilliant relationship with her mother who told her she trusted Sara implicitly. This made Sara determined to maintain that trust and was a great brake to us getting into mischief until we got engaged while away at university together. More on that later.

When I could not see Sara in person, I saw her on the TV. Yes, she was a star (at least in my eyes) on a children's show called

Nice One Stu.[6] The host played the naughty schoolboy who often delighted children and infuriated parents. He was a kind of antihero who taught young viewers the right way to do things by almost always getting it wrong himself. The show went through a period where Stu talked to a panel of teenagers in their last year of school. Of course, the very articulate future Mrs Carey was picked to be part of it.

Bearing in mind that no one much in New Zealand had digital or video recorders in 1977, I had to race home from work leaping between two buses, skidding into the house in time to turn on the telly in the hope that I would see Sara. This amused everyone who knew me but I was deadly serious about how important it was – my babe was influencing all of New Zealand's youth and children. I was so proud.

Well, time respects no man and Christmas came around all too soon when we had to say goodbye for a year. Sara was off to the US on a Rotary Exchange. Typical of Sara, she decided to apply when her friend told her about the idea. Despite her friend being turned down and Sara already having completed school, she won the heart of the local Rotary Club who made several special exceptions so she could go.

By now you will have figured that it was me who fell in love first. I plucked up the courage to tell her I loved her while at my parents' place in Napier. She was sitting on the swing chair in the backyard and I just blurted it out.

That was very courageous for me but instead of being met with a wonderful acknowledgement of reciprocated and undying love there was silence.

My heart skipped several beats as I waited. Eventually, she told me she didn't feel the same and in fact while she was away in the States she wanted the freedom to date others. It appeared that I had a real knack of getting into deteriorating situations with this girl – from bad to worse to unbelievably ghastly.

And so began lots of conversations about whether we should still be 'an item' while she took twelve months out to play the American field. I told her that going out with others was fine by me, but I knew that my heart would be the battered football in this game.

The day to say farewell came all too soon. We had her parents' house in Wellington to ourselves for the weekend. Thankfully we were joined by friends and we raided Pop's collection for a bottle of bubbly and had fish and chips on the beach together.

It was actually very romantic. Up until then we hadn't scored very highly in life's romance ratings.

The next day we said goodbye, me in love and her looking forward to exploring America and all it had to offer a beautiful seventeen-year-old girl from Downunder.

I needed to trust that if our relationship was from God then one day Sara would reciprocate my feelings. Like all young people I was in a hurry for love, but God wanted to do some serious work in my life first.

On that day, I could have wept that she didn't feel the same as me, and in fact I think I did.

Message to men (MTM)

How do you trust that God has a good plan for your life when everything around is screaming the opposite? We cry out to Him in prayer, sometimes day and night, only to see nothing change, not even a hint of progress.

Getting the right perspective is the first step towards unconditional trust. We are often blinded by the things right in front of us – our view obstructed by the proverbial trees of life, if you like. God sees the big picture, the whole plan, the layout of the woods and every detail in it.

Our life is valued, as seen through God's eyes, by the state of our heart. We are keenly interested in having our circumstances improve – He is just as keen to see our hearts transformed and for us to mature. We want circumstances to change, he wants circumstances to change us.

Take a step back, enjoy a moment to breathe and ask him not for material things but for his perspective. It will radically change your life and your marriage. Being a man of faith, who seeks God's ways over your own is a great foundation for love.

The Lord works out everything to its proper end …
Proverbs 16:4

Chapter Five
Absence Makes the Heart Ache

World Events

- World population reaches 4.3 billion – forty years later it is 7.7 billion
- The comic strip *Garfield* is debuted
- Space Invaders is released
- $100 in 1978 is worth over $380 in 2018
- Sara is in the United States for a year leaving me bereft

It started as a tough year without Sara. I was utterly miserable but I kept my argumentative skills honed by bickering with my older brother. Even that didn't help.

I longed to hear from Sara, often camping out by the letterbox even though I knew what time the postie came. But when I did get a letter, instead of joy my heart would sink. She was having a good time and went into detail about her dates with frisky Americans at her high school.

For me it was a no win – lonely and desperate to know what she was up to and then depressed when I found out. But God had some big things to do in my life that year. As it turned out, these were essential to finally winning the heart of my future wife.

My life had already done a major about turn. The previous year I had visited Sara's mum at her school. She was a new entrant teacher who loved children and was a natural at her job. Needless to say, I was inspired.

I was longing to spend my life doing something other than exploding plastic wine bags in a factory. There had to be a better use of what would take up a third of my life for the next forty years.

But there was a problem with applying to teachers' college. I was a hippie, a vegetarian and didn't have a decent set of clothes for the interview. What was worse was that I came from a working-class background where schooling was not highly regarded. I spoke 'funny', pronouncing 'th' as 'f'. The odds were stacked against me.

I wrestled with the idea of applying until it was almost too late. My overanalytical mind was at war with my faith. Eventually, I laid a Gideon's fleece[7] before God (not recommended). I asked him to give me three letters on the same day – one from Sara (she wrote every two to three days), one from an old girlfriend who was still mad at me and never wrote, and one from my ex-fiancé who definitely wanted nothing to do with me. It was a big ask. But my God is also big and very gracious to those who are desperate.

The allotted day came and I went eagerly to the letterbox. When I opened it out fell three letters from the three girls. I dropped to my knees and sobbed with joy that God loved me so much he would do this for me. How I loved him that day and how often I have looked back on that miracle and remembered how great my heavenly Dad is.

I borrowed some clothes and went to the interview. Of course, it was a disaster. The panel asked me things like, 'So what books are you reading at the moment?' 'The Bible,' I answered. 'And what else?' they continued. 'Just the Bible,' was my crisp reply.

I walked out knowing that it would take another major miracle for me to be accepted. Again, God rescued me and before I knew it, I was going to teachers' college. So this was what I was doing while Sara enjoyed her 'second' last year at school in a faraway country.

I visited her parents on Sara's eighteenth birthday and talked to her briefly on the phone. It was hard to really connect as we had her dad lurking in the background making unhelpful comments like, 'It's a bloody toll call and she is wasting it crying!'

My disposition deteriorated further as the year went on. It wasn't just the absence of Sara that left a hole in me. I had been a Christian for almost two years and devoured the Bible from cover to cover. I read about the miracles of God, the power in the name Jesus and the amazing works of the Holy Spirit. But I felt powerless and weak in my faith. It was like I was reading one thing but living a completely different way of life. I was not content with that and it really disturbed me.

Foolishly I was too busy to do anything about it. My life was full with writing long, deep letters to Sara, arguing with my older brother and trying my hardest to cope with the demands of teachers' college. Once again, God had to step in. This time it was in the form of an accident.

On a really windy day, I set off on my pushbike. Struggling to move forward I stood up from the seat to get more power. When I sat down the seat moved, pinging me abruptly in the testicles. Very suddenly I was in the worst pain I had ever experienced in my life. Somehow, I got back home and was driven to the hospital.

Once in Accident and Emergency I was told to take a seat and wait. Instead I violently threw up. Immediately I was put into a cubicle where I moaned in pain for forty-five minutes, thinking I was going to die. Eventually, the doctor came who pronounced that I had appendicitis and needed an operation. He turned to leave but didn't get far. I grabbed him by his white coat and told him through tears of pain and anger that it was my testicles.

Apparently, torsion of the testis is very serious and regarded as a surgical emergency. It certainly felt to me like it was a crisis. I was rushed under the knife and spent the next week recovering in hospital. To most of my friends it was a good laugh but God finally had my full attention. I used the many hours recuperating to read my Bible, to think and pray about my feeble Christian life – I wanted more.

One evening while lying on the hospital bed, I discussed this with my good friend. He suggested I visit this neat old couple in the church when I got out and could walk again (albeit lopsided for a while).

Eric and Veronica were indeed old, well into in their fifties. They had no children and were the most loving and patient people I had ever met. After taking a deep breath, I plunged in, telling them all about my frustrations, my weaknesses and how nothing seemed to add up.

Like all wise people, they listened intently. When I finally stopped raving at them, they continued to listen. Strange, I thought, maybe they had nodded off? The silence continued. I wasn't used to this as young people never leave a void in the conversation – it's be quick to talk or be ignored.

Eventually, Eric spoke. He simply said, 'You need to go on a New Life in the Spirit seminar' and gave me the details. I thought, that's it? Go on a seminar[8] run by the local Anglicans and everything will be alright? I walked out shaking my head about how strange this ancient couple seemed.

Little was I to know they would become like a spiritual mum and dad to me. What they modelled is still desperately needed in the Church today. Spiritual parenting is seriously lacking. In those days, I was more like an orphan than part of a wonderful big family, but God used this lesson in my life. During the last thirty-nine years, it has been prophesied[9] that I would be a father to many spiritual sons. This has been true and I have a long list of 'sons' whom I regard with great fondness.

I went along to these seminars and was completely baffled. People from many denominations were there to learn the truth about the Holy Spirit. In the late 1970s this was very new and more than a bit scary. The only reason I stayed was that it was very Bible-based and that appealed to me.

At the end of the course, we were asked to say whatever came into our minds as it often was the beginning of speaking in tongues. Slowly everyone began to speak a new language or utterance and there was great joy in the room for all – except me.

I had a word, but it sounded demonic and I refused to speak it. When the leader asked me to tell him the word, he laughed. He said it was an ancient word for God that he had come across when he was a missionary in India. In obedience, I spoke the word and was amazed at the flood that followed. I was speaking in tongues and didn't want it to end.

I didn't stop – I spoke in tongues in the shower, during my quiet times, while in the car (no more pushbiking for me) and at every opportunity I could. But that's not all, I began to get impressions and words of knowledge for people.[10] Those around me were amazed and wanted to know more. And thus, the movement of the Spirit began in our conservative Baptist Church. It didn't start with me but I was one of the more 'advanced'.

The joy of it was incredible as we witnessed people instantly set free from smoking addictions and saw swollen big toes healed in front of our eyes. Many of the words of knowledge were very intimate and brought significant breakthrough into people's lives. But all this came at a cost.

Our pastor experienced burnout so the youth pastor took over. His church was becoming divided and he didn't have the maturity to cope with it. Eventually he sat me down along with some of the other perpetrators and said it would be better if we left the church. His reasoning was that by raising hands during the worship we were making people uncomfortable. I was stunned but, as it turned out, this would not be the only time I would be asked to leave a church.

I plucked up the courage to write all this to Sara, thinking she would react in the same negative way. My letter started by saying I would not blame her if she wanted to call off our relationship but that I had been baptised in the Holy Spirit.[11] I told her the whole story and then spent a very nervous two weeks waiting for her reply.

I could hardly sleep as I worried about how she would take all this mysterious holy spooky stuff. Of course, she was over the moon. In fact, that letter sealed things between us and at that point she fell in love with me.

What had started as a year of absence causing great heartache had turned into something more precious than any other year of my life. I had found real power to live as a Christian and to do the works of God. I had also found my soulmate who shared the same deeply held views as me. I was ecstatic over all God had done for me. But there was much more to come before the year was out.

Message to men (MTM)

As men we like to be in control. We enjoy planning and prefer certainty over chaos. Well, I've got news for you. Not only are you not in control, but life with a wife by your side is very unpredictable.

Most likely on your wedding day you will pledge to love your spouse and acknowledge God as Lord of your newly founded household. Once the journey of marriage starts, these things will be sorely tested and, if you are wise, you will come to see that control is all but an illusion.

Many things will happen over the decades where your grip is deliberately loosened on life to teach you that God is at work and he is purposeful about refining your character and growing your faith.

The sooner you let go of being 'the boss of you' and partner up with your wife under the headship of a loving God, the more joy you will have that does not depend on outward circumstances.

The Lord directs our steps, so why try to
understand everything along the way?
Proverbs 20:24, NLT

Chapter Six
The Prodigal Returns

World Events

- Oil prices climb from around US$13 a barrel to US$32 following the Iranian revolution
- Sony Walkman releases portable audio cassette players
- China institutes the one child per family rule in 1979
- Sara returns from her year living overseas

It was a year of seemingly insurmountable problems coupled with amazing answers. By August we were both in love. Sara was nearly 14,000 kilometres away in Ohio. Although she would soon be back in Godzone (New Zealand) she was planning to go to Dunedin when she returned. Dunedin was the only place where she could study to be a dietician, which was her long-term dream.

It might as well have been America. It was at the south end of New Zealand on a different island. It would take days to drive there, but the expense of crossing Cook Strait would rule that option out for me anyway.

I naively thought I would transfer to the teachers' college in Dunedin. This was 1979 and most of the students at teachers' college were seventeen-year-old girls straight out of school. They had an unfortunate habit of falling in and out of love, so the colleges refused transfers unless you were married or engaged.

I, of course, was much more mature at twenty years of age. I didn't do such things. But the college would not budge.

In the end, the Dean said to me, 'Just say you are engaged, who's to know any different?' This was an opportunity to share my faith with her, which I did. To my surprise and delight it was well received by the Dean. But nothing changed.

I knew my relationship with Sara was already defying the odds. Everyone seemed to take great delight in telling us that long-distance relationships never work, especially those involving Rotary Exchanges.

I am not a patient person, but I am determined. Some call it stubborn. I knew that my love for Sara was more important than becoming a teacher and leaving behind the life of a factory worker on minimal wage. I went to the Dean and said I would resign if my transfer was not approved. I was going to Dunedin regardless.

When my case came up, they approved it without us being engaged. It seemed like the hand of God's favour was on me regarding teachers' college. The Dean said it was miracle and that she had never heard of this happening before. And with that opening we talked about God and miracles for a while.

All this time, I had kept everything about the transfer very quiet as I didn't want Sara to be under pressure or her parents to freak out. However, I was only putting off the inevitable.

Another momentous Christmas came around and I travelled to Auckland to meet Sara. Her parents had moved to a lovely spot in Auckland called Titirangi. Its Māori meaning is 'fringe of heaven'. I had bought a new shirt to wear and a large red rose for Sara. Then the bad news came.

Sara was flying out of Chicago but was caught in a massive blizzard regarded as one of the three worst ever to strike that city. She was stuck – no way in or out for days. Added to this was that she was unable to contact us.

Each day, Lesley washed and ironed my special shirt and cut a little off the stem of my rose. I then drove twenty minutes to the airport to meet every plane from America that landed. Day after day there was no Sara. Tensions mounted in the household. It seemed that Pop was not happy with me gatecrashing and was furious that Sara might hug me before any other family member.

Just when my rose was beginning to look very short and my shirt not so new, we got a phone call from Sara. She was in LA with a millionaire Rotarian who was doing his best to try to get her on a flight out. Since Chicago is a major hub, the planes had banked up for days. It wasn't as simple as just getting on the next plane to New Zealand. Once more we had to wait.

I tried to help by avoiding Pop, especially when I flooded the laundry by leaving my socks in the laundry tub. It seemed as though I could do no right in his eyes. Finally, another phone call. Sara was arriving the next day.

We all went to the airport, but you could have cut the air with a samurai sword. To my surprise as the plane landed Pop went for a walk and was nowhere to be seen. But that wasn't the only surprise.

My lovely Sara had bright red hair and now weighed more than I did. I didn't care. I had her back in my arms.

Luckily for us all, Sara's brother, Simon, jumped the barrier and was first to hug her. The drama was over for now.

Back at the house, I gave her my presents. There were twelve gifts for each of the days of Christmas. They were numbered and the very last one was 'Me in Dunedin with you'. She was thrilled and let out a whoop of delight. By contrast, her parents were stunned and very unhappy.

They somehow failed to realise that most girlfriends and boyfriends live in the same city. To be fair, they were hoping that this relationship would fade and that this hippie would hop off somewhere far away.

On reflection, I can't really blame them. Lesley was frightened of me because I was so intense. Being a vegetarian and a fundamentalist Christian did not win me any friends except for Sara. Pop was very worried that Sara was getting involved with a working-class lad who didn't really have much to offer his precious only daughter. He was protecting her in his own way.

Years later, when I had a daughter of my own, I understood those strong protective feelings fathers have towards their children.

The next year in Dunedin was just as eventful as the previous two.

Message to men (MTM)

We operate our lives by making quick judgements, often based on first impressions which are not always correct. I was the victim of that sort of thinking but in retrospect, and now as a father of a beautiful daughter, I can see the reasoning behind it. As the old saying goes, there are always two sides to the story.

Sara and I could not see the limitations and dangers of being in love so young, or the potential problems that inevitably arose from our backgrounds being worlds apart. We faced many challenges to complete our studies and make a go of being adults who were able stand on their own two feet.

Her parents failed to grasp the potential we had and the amazing commitment we felt towards each other to make this work. They saw a perfect storm, we just saw each other and a God who promised to made our love strong.

Quick judgements are a part of everyday life, but harm comes when we refuse to change our assumptions and admit we were wrong. There are two sides to every story and a wise husband and parent will try to see all points of view and seek to test assumptions before settling fast on shaky conclusions.

The first speech in a court case is always convincing – until the cross-examination starts!
Proverbs 18:17, *The Message*

Chapter Seven
Dunners

World Events

- The Sahara Desert experiences snow for thirty minutes
- First snowboard commercially available
- In New Zealand, the average wage is $157 per week
- I head to Dunedin and Sara joins me

In February 1979, I crammed all my belongings into the car and drove to Dunedin. I was free at last from the confines of the past and was looking forward to being together with the girl of my dreams.

Dunedin is a university city and is known as the 'Edinburgh of the South'. The houses are brick which is unusual in an earthquake-prone country like New Zealand. Dunners, as it is fondly known as by the student population, enjoys bracingly cold weather typical of its namesake.

It was not unheard of to find someone in a kilt on a frosty corner playing the bagpipes when the rest of us were scurrying from heater to heater and avoiding the great outdoors. I love the place, but can't figure why it was the biggest city in New Zealand until 1900.

After a very long boat trip and drive I arrived in mini-Scotland in my new car, bewildered and not knowing a soul. The old hotted-up Cortina had sadly died so I had bought the model up, the Mark III. It had a normal exhaust and standard engine so Sara was not that impressed, secretly thinking it was more of an old man's car, suitable for someone in their thirties.

My destination was Simpson House – the old and cold two-storey accommodation for Baptist students. I was the first of the intake to arrive and so took the best room. It had its own fireplace, which was quaint I thought. Little did I know it would be my saviour during the icy Dunedin winters – not to mention the freezing springs and autumns.

One by one my four new flatmates arrived. We were an interesting group; a medical student who never felt the cold – if it was really bad, he would just roll down his sleeves. A dental student who had a real human skull in his room. A political science student who liked cigars and a good debate. And for a while the other 'flattie' was a surveying student until he took the plunge and got married. He was replaced by a pastor's son, who was wild and not housetrained.

Sara arrived by plane and we were finally together in the same city after fourteen months apart. The joy of it was unbelievable. I met her at the airport in my 'old man's car' and then took her to Unicol Hostel which consisted of two twin towers. These fortresses were mainly filled with first-year students who went mad with the freedom of being away from home. Food fights were commonplace, especially if the general populous took exception to the evening meals, which happened with remarkable frequency. Pots of yogurt were the main weapon of choice and boy, could they make a mess. The place was crazy and I didn't like Sara staying there.

She didn't like it much either and spent a lot of time at my flat. Lonny's cooking night was a highlight for the lads as Sara was in charge and she was a great cook. My flatties didn't know what to do with a vegetarian and so the standard meal for me was a very rubbery omelette. I coped, but what I didn't like was the house rule that the cook did not have to clean up. It meant that when we were rostered on dishes, the rest of the night was dedicated to nothing else as these boys seemed to use and abuse every pot in the house.

It felt good to be in Dunedin, especially since Sara was with me. We quickly settled into a routine of seeing each other every moment we could in between classes and study. We were in love.

One of the first things we tried to do was to find a church. Obviously, living in Baptist accommodation we thought we should try the Baptist church. However, this sterile and unfriendly place immediately ousted us six students when we all sat down in the pews dedicated to the families who had bought them. We were hustled out of the seats and never went back. One of our number had heard of a church for 'students' so we went along to the Apostolic Church. This place knew how to welcome young people and so we stayed.

We grew to love the old pastor despite his many foibles. When praying for people, the pastor would place his hand on your head and shake it violently until your jaw hurt. He was also the most tone-deaf person I have ever met – he loved to break into song, expecting others to somehow follow along. It was painful to witness. Even so, the man's heart was good and he and his wife became like parents to the hundreds of young people under their care.

By April that year, Sara and I had gone from being in love to being insanely in love. One evening, after we had been volunteer ushers at the Korean Girls' Choir, we went for a walk in the rain. We walked through the Botanical Gardens in the dark, soaking wet but not caring at all.

Standing on a bridge I said to Sara, 'I am lost.' She queried why and I answered, 'I am at a loss as to know when we should get married.' She took this as a proposal, which it was, and said yes. Sara had just turned nineteen and I wasn't even twenty-one. That was a minor point to two rain-soaked romantics.

It wasn't a minor point to her parents…

Message to men (MTM)

Sometimes we dream of new beginnings, a fresh start – then everything will be OK and all our problems sorted. One of life's not so little jokes is that we often take our problems with us no matter where we go.

Initially, being in Dunedin was wonderful without the agony of being apart. But despite the temporary state of romantic bliss, we hadn't reached heaven yet. Sara and I had plenty to sort out. The Lord had work to do in us and he hasn't stopped in nearly four decades of marriage.

Men, don't be fooled by placing your confidence in new things. Your problems are often deep-rooted and not as easily solved as you may think. We mustn't sell our soul to things that mask the real issues we face. Instead, we need to pin our hope on God as the master craftsman of our life, not on better circumstances or new opportunities.

Since we are his delight, the apple of his eye, our Father will not let us settle for less than the best and that starts and finishes with the state of our soul.

My child, don't reject the Lord's discipline, and don't be upset when
he corrects you. For the Lord corrects those he loves,
just as a father corrects a child in whom he delights.
Proverbs 3:11-12, NLT

Chapter Eight
Mischief in the Air

World Events

- Visicalc, the first spreadsheet software, is introduced
- Margaret Thatcher becomes Britain's first woman Prime Minister
- In NZ, the Carless days scheme is introduced in response to the second oil shock
- Sara and I are struggling with being engaged

We were engaged and there was mischief in the air. The first naughty thing I did was to borrow the money from Sara to buy her a ring. Technically, the money came from her father, who was supporting Sara through university that year. I did eventually pay her back, but only confessed the sneaky transaction to Pop decades after the event.

Next, we agreed to keep our betrothal secret until she had spoken to her parents. This was never going to happen as good news is like a wild cat. It can't be herded or kept in the bag and before a day had gone by, the news had spread.

It was a bit of a shock to most. We were still young and very poor, with years of study ahead of us. But we were in love and as Christians we didn't want to slip up by sleeping with each other before we got married. Why wait? we thought. Love was everything and anything else was a minor detail.

How differently we think now. Getting married when one or both of you is a teenager is high risk but we weren't the first of our friends to go down this path. Some of the marriages survived, others collapsed, but all went through rocky times. Frequently babies arrived early on. If that was not tricky enough, most of the couples did not truly discover who they were as people until well into their twenties.

So here we were, engaged at nineteen and twenty, far from home and without anyone to hold us accountable. But first we had to face Sara's parents. Sara rang them and it did not go well. During the term break she flew to Auckland to discuss things face-to-face while her coward of a fiancé found some urgent assignment he had to do in Dunedin.

The conversation was heated to say the least. Pop shouted at Sara that he didn't like me, and he could not change. Being a feisty and confident young woman, Sara stood her ground insisting that he would have to change as we were going ahead regardless and didn't need his permission.

In fact, Pop and Lesley did get right behind the wedding. It was a remarkable turnaround and testimony to how love can change someone. They never brought up their disapproval again and were 100 per cent supportive of the wedding. I joined them in Auckland once the shouting had subsided.

Sara, Lesley and I then drove to Napier to tell my parents, me squashed in the back of the minivan while the girls took turns driving. When we finally arrived, we held up Sara's hand to show my mum the ring. 'That's nice dear, I do love your jersey,' was her response. It was a flat occasion to say the least.

Back in Dunedin, Sara and I had a huge amount of learning to do about being 'adults' in love. When she wasn't visiting me at my flat, I was in her room at Unicol. We befriended the Unicol cleaner and had some deep discussions, particularly when she saw we were engaged. Dirty socks under the bed had been the death knell to her own relationship and she was desperate to stop us making the same mistakes she had made.

We thought this very sad, and made a pact to actively deal with the issues that bothered one another. Being considerate over the little things makes a big difference in a marriage. It's a vivid indicator to the other person of how much you respect them and what they value.

This led to a mind shift in our opinion towards equity in marriage. When a whole is divided evenly it turns into two halves. Your share and my share of things becomes the yardstick by which we judge each other's performance as a spouse.

The better way is to give and to serve each other. Instead of weakening the partnership bond through entitlement, it is strengthened through kindness. This was a grand idea, but the reality of it was to bite us many times before becoming foundational in our marriage.

Once it was official that we were engaged, the brakes came off. We found we were incredibly passionate towards each other and constantly struggled to stay pure. The Bible, in 1 Timothy 5:2, teaches men that purity dictates they should treat young women as sisters. I guess that didn't help me. I had no sisters.

We spent hours cuddled up together by my little fireplace. We warmed our way through the winter using wood from the house next door that had burnt to the ground the year before. Too much cuddling and smooching was not good so we went for long walks and talks.

Probably the only thing that saved us was a discussion we had one night when I told Sara that if we slipped up and went the whole way, I would marry her the next day without a wedding ceremony. Finally, we had some sort of brake even if it was more handbrake than full ABS disc system.

We really didn't have anyone to talk to. We tried to befriend some of the married couples in the church, but they were busy coping with children and the busyness of life themselves. We were so in love that we were insular, but desperately in need of advice and a watchful eye from those more mature than we were.

What was missing was pre-marriage training and accountability. Like most couples in the 1970s and today, our time and effort was spent on the wedding rather than what happens afterwards. Hours and hours were poured into getting those few moments on the big day perfect without a thought for the years that were ahead.

Our experience is one of the main reasons Sara and I run pre-marriage and marriage courses today. Back then we were infatuated with each other, but needed to learn to love. Relationships are complicated and couples must be equipped for what they will face together if they are to beat the odds and stay together.

That year passed and we survived by the skin of our teeth. I was about to turn the grand old age of twenty-one so we went to Palmerston North for my coming of age party. It wasn't a great academic year for my very intelligent fiancé – too many distractions and not enough focus on the right things.

Like all years, it soon came to an end. I stayed in Dunedin and worked as a truckers' off-sider delivering bulk groceries to stores.

Sara went to Auckland and worked at a department store for the impressive total of a dollar per hour. Despite not rolling in the money, I managed to buy a number of things for our future life together. The warehouse had all sorts of goodies heavily discounted for staff. One of my strategic purchases was two identical shiny ten-speed bikes with mudguards and basket carriers. This was to be our only mode of transport for the next two years.

In between driving around Dunedin as king of the road in a truck, I found a one-bedroom flat on George Street just up from the university. With the help of my church home group we set about cleaning it and painting the disgusting cupboards. Once done, it looked just perfect for a newly married couple. When I proudly showed a picture of Sara to the landlady, she was surprised and commented that she looked about seventeen. I was indignant and blurted out: 'No, she's nineteen.'

We had no idea how young we were or what we were taking on. But God did and I am so grateful for that.

Message to men (MTM)

Despite being in a great church, Sara and I were largely isolated. There was no one close who could take us under their wing and provide us with wise counsel.

Over the years, Sara and I have witnessed many young, in love Christian couples ruin their faith through becoming insular and refusing correction. Often this is through inappropriate and premature sexual behaviour.

Our natural tendency as blokes is to be self-made men where we see admitting we need help as weakness. In life, wisdom comes from surrounding ourselves with others who can challenge us and keep us accountable.

Males don't always like that but this is God's way. He uses other men to sharpen us when we become blunt and he ignites us with the fire of others when we begin to fizzle.

This also applies to our personal life and that of our marriage. To misquote the saying, it takes a community to raise a good marriage.

In the wild, the isolated are picked off by predators. As Christians we are a community of believers where there is genuine strength –so let's start acting that way.

Get all the advice and instruction you can,
so you will be wise the rest of your life.
Proverbs 19:20

Chapter Nine
The Big Day

1 . JAN . 1980

World Events
- Sixty-four guests arrive from all over New Zealand
- It's a Tuesday and the world stops while Sara and I get married

Dr Seuss once commented, 'People are weird. When we find someone with weirdness that is compatible with ours, we team up and call it love.' Our big day arrived and it was both weird and wonderful at the same time.

In the lead up to the wedding, the Carey lads drove to Napier for Christmas. Unfortunately, my mum was going through one of her bouts of illness. The two of us chatted for a bit about the wedding and I casually asked where she was staying. Shocked, she said, 'With Sara's parents, of course.' Equally surprised, I asked if that had been arranged, to which she said 'No, but surely Pop and Lesley would have us stay, we are the groom's parents.'

I tried to explain that they had only one spare bedroom and that it was being used as part of the reception. The conversation turned surreal as she became indignant about this, stating firmly that if that was the case then she and Dad were not coming.

Unbeknown to me an aunty stepped in and cajoled Mum into turning up by paying for them to have a motel nearby. This aunty and her husband were later to become Christians. On the day of the wedding, Mum was wearing a flamboyant red outfit that made her look like a gypsy and Dad was attired in his best T-shirt. What was even weirder was that although Dad came to the wedding ceremony, he failed to turn up at the reception. Being a keen fisherman, he instead took the opportunity to look at boats in the Auckland harbour. Dad has a dislike of crowds, as he is deaf; it was probably to his advantage as there would have been a choice few words aimed at him that night from my mum.

The wedding party was largely a family affair and we were billeted out to friendly neighbours. While I was eating breakfast on the morning of the big day, my younger brother, Vic, burst into the house to show me a rash that had appeared covering his entire back. He paced up and down with nerves, wondering what to do while I calmly finished my toast. Vic was my best man and the stress of it was beginning to show.

Sara and I had planned the wedding to be on the first day of the new year of the new decade; 1 January 1980. The wedding was to be simple but with a few twists. Since almost every one of our sixty-four guests had travelled to be there, we wanted to greet them at the door of the church to thank them for coming long distances. My older brother had different ideas.

He was the photographer and held the firm belief that the bride must be late to the church. Sara was intending to be early but unknown to me, my brother deliberately kept taking photographs. All our poor guests had to amuse themselves outside the church while I diligently guarded the entrance. By the time Sara arrived in the family Mini, adorned with a bridal teddy on the bonnet, I was beside myself. The first thing I said to Sara on seeing her was, 'You're bloody late.' That precious moment when the groom first sees his bride in all her beauty had vanished.

Luckily for me, Sara was gracious about it and we proceeded to greet our bewildered guests as they filed into the tiny Old Soldiers and Sailors Memorial Church. Once they were all inside, my mum and dad escorted me down the aisle and then Sara's parents did the same for her.

More photographs followed, but I am not sure I smiled much at the person behind the camera. I was still cross with him.

Everything about the wedding was delightfully unpretentious. Sara's dress was handmade and really suited her. The cake was baked by her aunty and decorated by Sara in the shape of a Horn of Plenty. The reception was at Pop and Lesley's tiny but funky Lockwood house. It had a big deck overlooking a forest of endless green with a small window to the sea below. Pop had earlier reinforced the deck – just in case the guests ate too much.

The only real extravagance was the use of professional caterers. We had had tasters of the different courses prior to the wedding so knew that the food was divine. The risky decision was to allow the caterer to choose the wine list. This proved a disaster. We were given several bottles for our honeymoon and had to add lemonade to it before we could drink it. The deal was that Pop paid for any opened bottles, but the caterer had uncorked dozens that the guests understandably had not drunk. Pop still talks about this decades years later.

The time came for speeches and everyone else did well with lots of laughter. I had tried to prepare a speech beforehand but writer's block had got to me so I decided to wing it. When I got up to talk, my mind went blank and I stumbled through probably one of the worst groom's speeches of the last century. Thank goodness that in those days no one videoed the event. I learned that day that I am not a natural public speaker; since then I have always prepared well in advance.

Once all the formal stuff was over, Sara and I silently slipped away to get changed into our casual clothes. I had worn a suit but a tie was a step too far for this ex-hippie. When we emerged, everyone was lined up expecting us to leave. 'No, no,' we protested, 'we just want to enjoy the rest of the day.' But it was too late. The lads grabbed me, turned me upside down and poured ice, rice and confetti down my trousers before we were manhandled out the door.

A friend and his wife had lent us their old Morris 1100. It was gutless but to us it was one of the best gifts ever. We were propelled into the waiting not-so-limo and after some quick and tearful goodbyes we were on our way to a lifetime of new adventures.

Message to men (MTM)

We approached our wedding and both sets of parents were not happy with us. Some of the reasoning was valid, some was not. The lesson here is to be discerning with your children and your wife over what to make a stand over.

Men too often 'put their foot down' as a sign of strength and as a statement of being in control rather than through wisdom and love. Once done, we can be too proud to retract our stance or even, God forbid, say we are sorry.

The result can be to drive those we love away from us, especially if we make them choose between their future spouse and us. Foolishly, we seem to believe we are always right and that those close to us will choose us over others.

Who knows what my relationship with my mother would have been like if she had not come to my wedding, or with Sara's parents had they refused to get behind the wedding day.

So, men, choose wisely when you puff yourself up and dance your manly rant. The consequences can be long-lasting.

The tongue has the power of life and death …
Proverbs 18:21

Chapter Ten
Zens is Not a Word

World Events

- The Rubik's Cube makes its international debut at the British Toy and Hobby Fair
- Average life expectancy in NZ is 72.8 years old. Thirty-eight years later it is 82.2 years old
- As far as Sara and I are concerned, nothing is happening throughout the rest of the world as we are on our honeymoon

That New Year's Day of 1980 we drove through a tropical rainstorm and a few minutes later through blazing sunshine. It was mid-summer and hot. My tired bride was lying, dozing on my lap while I navigated the trip to the wonderful Bay of Islands. The problem was that the trip took four hours and we were exhausted after the Big Day. In retrospect, not the smartest thing to do.

When we finally got there, we realised that we had been shoved out of the door before we were ready and had left behind the address where we were staying. Instantly we went from bliss to a sinking feeling of despair.

Sara's parents had generously paid for us to stay a week in the bottom flat of a beach house. But without a mobile phone in those days it was no easy task to contact them in order to find the missing address – we needed a payphone and lots of coins. I thought I could remember the street name so we found the nearest thing.

We then cruised up and down, looking for the place that best fitted the description we had pieced together from memory. Once the target was reached, I then proceeded to deploy my skills from a misspent youth and broke into the flat. Fortunately, I did no real damage and to my relief found a welcome note on the side table to 'Mr and Mrs Carey'. I could so easily have been arrested on my honeymoon and spent the night in jail rather than with my lovely bride.

Overcome by hunger after the long trip and the relief of finding the right place, we then set off to get some food. Since fish and chips on the beach the night before Sara left for the United States had been so romantic we decided to repeat the occasion. Sara went into the shop full of people and it was all she could do not to shout at the top of her voice that she had got married that day. Couldn't people see that for themselves?

After our delicious meal, the 'what next' question hung silently in the air. I said I was going to have a shower and that she could join me if she wanted but absolutely no pressure. To my delight, she appeared undressed, all meek and slightly embarrassed. We kissed and cuddled in the shower but didn't have enough experience of techniques to go beyond that. We didn't want the shower to end as we were so enjoying each other's naked bodies.

Eventually it finished by itself when the water went cold. We thought no more about it until the next day when there was a knock on the door from the people above. They pleaded with us not to use all the hot water as the tank serviced both halves of the house. Oops.

That night we gently made love and cuddled for ages, happy to be in each other's arms without feeling guilty or longing to be married.

Later as we drifted off to sleep, I had a horrific nightmare. I had been plagued by demonic nightmares all my life, seeing terrible things in the room with my eyes wide open.

My new wife, of incredible faith, announced right there and then that we weren't going to put up with this and we prayed together. She forcefully claimed the promise found in Matthew 18:19 that when two believers agree in Jesus' name it will be done and demanded that the nightmares be gone, never to return. And as simple as that, they went.

Many years later, I can say it is a miracle that I have never had another nightmare like those unwelcome invaders which had frequented my sleep for twenty-one years.

The honeymoon was fun. We lay on the beach and sunbathed or read books and played Scrabble. Once when tanning our bodies on a magnificent beach, a child of about seven came over and said she had a song for us. It went: 'Fatty and Skinny up a tree, K.I.S.S.I.N.G.' I was very slim in those days and Sara was still losing the extras pounds she had acquired in the US. We laughed as it didn't really worry us, we were so happy just to be there and with each other.

The Scrabble, however, was a different story. Sara was quick-minded and equipped with a huge vocabulary. I was slower, both in finding the right words but also in making sure they earned maximum points. Sara would become bored, which was a perfect tactic of mine; she would agree to anything to keep the game moving.

After scoring a beautifully placed ZEN, I then added an 'S' to make it ZENS which resulted in the first-ever blistering argument of our married life.

People had been very generous to us and we had just enough money from gifts to go on the Champagne Cruise around the amazing Bay of Islands. The brochure said something similar to the internet version today:

> On your dream-come-true cruise around the Bay of Islands you'll discover uninhabited sanctuary islands, watch dolphins at play, visit fascinating historic places and enjoy the finest gourmet cuisine served with endless sea views.[12]

And it was wonderful, but several things struck us that day. We were the only ones on the boat to swim in the crystal-clear blue waters and hardly anyone else was cuddly or talking to each other. We discussed these observations that evening over a glass of wine and lemonade resolving never to let our love change to be like that. Having fun together was an essential ingredient to keeping love alive and vibrant.

Having a car was fantastic as I had sold mine some time before the wedding. It brought us the freedom to cruise around sightseeing; we even picked up a girl who had nowhere to stay. Naturally, we let her stay the night on the floor of our little flat. After all that's the sort of thing you do on a honeymoon – isn't it?

Eventually, our time was up and Sara's parents and brother, Simon, arrived as they were making use of the place for a few days while we returned to Dunedin. I don't know how but we all managed to squeeze into the flat that night. Somehow, it seemed normal to share our honeymoon with others.

The best part of the honeymoon for me was falling asleep cuddling and then waking up in each other's arms. That way we both ended and started the day thinking about each other.

This was love as expressed once more by Dr Seuss when he said: 'You know you're in love when you can't fall asleep because reality is finally better than your dreams.'

I had married the girl of my dreams and still think that way nearly four decades later.

Message to men (MTM)

Is your wife your best friend? Is she the first person you think of when you want to do something fun? Do you have common interests and shared hobbies?

There is a saying that families that play together, stay together. It's the same for marriages. Having fun is an essential component of growing close to each other.

Don't let the years take the shine off that. Be deliberate in building great memories as a couple, where there is plenty of laughter and enjoyment together. Otherwise when the kids are gone, or when you retire and suddenly have loads of time, you will wonder, 'Who is this stranger I am married to? Do I really like them?'

Marriage is the long game with rewards beyond anything else. Just like on the honeymoon, make sure you continue to cherish your bride as your best friend and companion.

Let your wife be a fountain of blessing for you. Rejoice in the wife of your youth ... May you always be captivated by her love.
Proverbs 5:18-19, NLT

Chapter Eleven
Changes Afoot

World Events
- Robert Mugabe wins the election in Zimbabwe
- We face weekly expenses of $30 rent and $20 food
- Pac-Man is released
- Sara and I are struggling to adapt to marriage

It's not that Sara and I were made for each other, it's more that we were *being* made for each other. We were a 'work in progress' and as such, our first year of marriage brought much change to our lives. Was it a shock? Yes. Was it fun? Yes. Would I change anything about it? Absolutely – I would change me.

Now that the honeymoon was over, we had a borrowed car to return. Sounds easy, but this was when we struck our first big challenge as a married couple. It was January 1980 and New Zealand was in the middle of a petrol crisis.

Car drivers were required to refrain from using their car on one day of the week, as designated by the owner. Each car displayed a coloured sticker on its windscreen which noted the day on which it could not be used. Added to this foolishness was a restriction on the hours that petrol could be sold.[13]

On that day, we set off down the North Island of New Zealand, blissfully unaware that we were heading for trouble. However, when it came to filling up with petrol we discovered that all the petrol stations had closed five minutes earlier.

Our petrol gauge was getting perilously close to empty. What could we do? We contacted the owner of the car who told us that his brother's farm was not far from our southward route.

We winged it on much prayer and the smell of an oily rag while we drove deep into the countryside. Tensions rose in the car but were matched with increasingly fervent prayer. Much to our delight and amazement we found Farmer Giles. He was just as surprised, but happily filled our tank from his reserves.

It seemed like the miracles were endless in those days. However, it did leave a lasting impact on us – both Sara and I hate having less than quarter of a tank of petrol in the car and tend to fret if it ever hits lower than that.

It's funny how things that happened back then set the pattern of our behaviour for years to come. When we got to Otaki we stayed at Sara's matron of honour's house. Early the next morning, her best friend, Diana, came in for a chat. Sara climbed out of bed and in doing so whipped the blankets off me exposing my nakedness for all to see. I was mortified and even now, many years later, prefer to sleep in my boxers for safety's sake (we live in a land of earthquakes, don't you know).

Our wedding presents had been hauled south by several kind friends, so we borrowed large suitcases and piled them so full that we had to sit on them to make them close. When we got to the bus station, the driver shook his head and said that there was no way he could take that many huge and heavy suitcases.

I just wanted to punch him and force my way onto the bus. My cunning wife stepped in with the flutter of her eyelashes and said, 'Oh, but we are on our honeymoon and these are our wedding presents for our new life together.' Of course, Sara's charm paid off and we were soon sitting happily on the bus cuddled up together, safe in the knowledge that our suitcases were cruising along with us on our way to Dunedin.

When we got to our new home I, being the romantic one in the marriage, decided to carry my wife up the narrow flight of stairs. She was heavier than me and the stairs were very steep. With Sara protesting and giggling the whole way, I staggered up one step at a time until we reached the top. Exhausted, I then realised I also had a large number of heavy suitcases which required carrying up and across the threshold. That was nowhere near as romantic or as much fun.

Our flat was tiny with a narrow kitchen that led out to a small balcony, a hallway with freezer and washing machine in it, a lounge with a broken couch that ate visitors who dared to sit on it and a small table in the bay window. The bedroom was an 'L' shape but big enough for two desks and a bed. The bathroom was fireman red with a shower over a deep, lovely bath; ideal for newlyweds.

We soon had our share of mishaps at the flat. First, while playing king of the castle we broke the bed. No one even to this day believes that we were just being silly and not embraced in violent love-making. But that's the truth. As a result, we slept on that mattress on the floor for two years.

After we had been married for a few weeks I encountered the ultimate difference between men and women. In the middle of the night I staggered out to the toilet, and as I climbed wearily back into bed, I must have woken Sara as she followed suit.

Just as I was happily drifting back off to sleep, I was sharply awakened by a thump on my shoulder (it's never been right since). Expecting to see a burglar or the beginning of the Third World War I leapt up to discover I was standing face-to-face with a very angry new bride who had fallen into the toilet bowl.

You see, ladies do not need to put the light on when doing a quick 3 a.m. wee but are prone to such misfortunes as 'Attacks of Cold Porcelain' when their husbands leave the seat up. Needless to say, I was quickly trained in the art of putting the seat down, but not the lid as that could be equally disastrous.

We loved to take long baths together. The one luxury we had in those days was a telephone and on this particular night while we were in the bath it rang and rang without ceasing. Annoyed and thinking it was someone wanting us on some trifling matter, I climbed out of the bath and walked over to the phone leaving a trail of soggy footprints.

The caller was the landlady who lived below, desperately asking what we were doing as water was streaming down her walls. The bath was so full that water was pouring down the overflow, which in an old house had long since ceased to be connected.

Despite minor mishaps, Sara and I loved our tiny haven. We had little in the way of money or possessions, but needed very little to survive. Our biggest treat was buying a pack of liquorice off-cuts once a week and playing cards together. I still love

70

liquorice as an indulgence and even to this day can't figure how students ever afford a lifestyle of booze and extravagance.

We were poor but happy. Sara had become a vegetarian like me. Our meals were entirely homemade and simple. We made our own bread, grew bean sprouts and brewed ginger beer. We had several brand-new rubbish bins full of beans and ingredients so we could live as cheaply as possible.

Sara's vegetarianism lasted for about a year, until she started dreaming of liver and decided to go back to eating meat.

We changed a lot that year. These days, Sara and I often observe how some couples enter marriage thinking they can change each other for the better. Change does happen and if the marriage is a good one then there will be lots of adjustments. But the twist is that you are the one who must change for the better. It's not possible to change the other person – all good change starts with you.

Barack Obama once said: 'Change will not come if we wait for some other person or some other time. We are the ones we've been waiting for. We are the change that we seek.'[14]

Message to men (MTM)

We spend a third of our lives at work. To be promoted we must continually adapt our behaviour and modify our thinking, getting to grips with the latest innovation. These days, work is all about challenge and change. Progress only comes when we improve our skills, broaden our experience and embrace new things.

We see this as an absolute priority in the workplace, so why not in our marriage? Our approach to the most important relationship on earth should be no different than our approach to our careers.

In life, success comes through change. Just as you wouldn't be lazy at work, don't be lazy in love. Earning money, not cheating on your wife and playing with the kids is not enough to keep a marriage alive. To mature in love and life, you must constantly work at it.

> *Intelligent people are always ready to learn.*
> *Their ears are open for knowledge.*
> Proverbs 18:15, NLT

Chapter Twelve
Imperfect People

World Events

- CNN is launched, the world's first twenty-four-hour international television news channel
- The United States leads a boycott of the Olympic Games in Moscow to protest Soviet invasion of Afghanistan. Twenty-one years later, the USA also invades Afghanistan
- John Lennon is shot twice in the back and dies
- Otago University moves from punch cards to allowing students evening access to the mainframe resulting in me often working through the night

Nicky Gumbel said: 'A true relationship is two imperfect people who refuse to give up on each other.'[15]

Our first year of marriage was fun but difficult. There was no doubt we were in love, but we had a lot of adjustment to make. We certainly weren't perfect.

The romantic antics that come with a whirlwind engagement had tended to suppress our propensity to fight. But now that we had all that we longed for, the gloves were off.

It's amazing how we didn't understand each other and how often we thought there was some sinister motive behind the other's action or words.

Early on, we had friends over for dinner. While I entertained our guests in the lounge, Sara was in our separate little kitchen cooking up a storm, not only on the stove but in her head. I was oblivious to my wife's anger.

After the delicious main course, Sara demanded that I do the coffee and dessert as she had done everything else without my help.

I reacted, and stood my ground. As the head of the new household, I was determined to assert my authority, and so we argued in front of our guests showing little restraint. I am pretty sure they zipped off early that night.

Interestingly, since that time we have always hated kitchens that isolate the cook. We prefer an open plan design where everyone can be sociable while the meal is being prepared.

Hospitality has become a huge part of who we are and what we love doing. Our approach nowadays is to see it as a partnership where we seek to serve each other and our guests.

This was a stressful year for us both. Even though we were so young, we were made assistant house group leaders in the church.

Most of the group were in their thirties or forties and soon into the year, the leader began to do shift work, forcing us to lead the group by default. At least Sara had turned twenty, so she was no longer a teenager.

Without fail Sara and I would argue just before the house group met. We would then attempt to lead a group of oldies into deeper spiritual truths while trying to conceal our ill feeling toward each other.

It was not uncommon for conflict to arise before a stressful event. This was a pattern we observed again years later when we had kids.

The church back then did not understand the principle of the Marriage Year, as found in Deuteronomy 24:5. This basically states: 'If a man has recently married, he must not be sent to war or have any other duty laid on him. For one year he is to be free to stay at home and bring happiness to the wife he has married.'

I am not sure how much happiness I brought my wife that year; there were many other stresses on our lives at that time, mainly caused by me.

For starters, I was doing two concurrent degrees while trying to finish teachers' college. To complete my science degree I had to pad it out with things like Stage 2 Botany which involved endless labs where we classified different species of plants. It was a boring class for everyone so I spent most of the time debating evolution with my classmates and the tutors. They enjoyed goading me but I also relished the open discussions about Jesus. I was useless at botany and half way through the year, the university wrote to teachers' college saying that they thought I would fail and that I should withdraw from the course.

Just when I was seriously thinking that the university had a point, one of my classmates asked to talk to me in private. It turned out that Chris had been intently listening to the debates.

As a 'straight A student', it wasn't the strength of my argument that had impressed him, it was the way I conducted myself. I took the discussions in good humour and never used the situation to make personal attacks or to demean the opposition. I was obviously better at arguing with others than I was with my wife.

I led Chris to the Lord on that day, which was one of the most joyous occasions of my life. Chris and I would regularly meet together, where I would teach him about the Bible and God and in return he would tutor me in botany. When the final practical exam came around, he scored a predictable A+ and me a B+. It was a shock to the university and to teachers' college but most of all to me.

The main stress that year was the Computer Science major I was doing. The first semester involved the use of punch cards where a machine created little holes in large cards. Once done, we had to carry them to the computer suite, being extra careful not to drop them, and submit them for reading. Several hours later, we would get a print-out saying 'syntax error' and have to start again.

But that was not the source of the stress. The university upgraded its mainframes to include green screen terminals which second and third year students could use after 8 p.m. and before 8 a.m. the next day. I would load up with thermos flasks of coffee and settle down for night after night of programming. This was the only way to get through the work. Many a time I came home as the birds were singing, only to crawl into bed for a couple of hours of sleep before my first lecture.

What I didn't realise was that I had developed an addiction to coffee. Years later, when drinking too much coffee was identified as bad for you, I discovered that I was having an average of twelve cups per day.

With so much caffeine in my bloodstream it's miraculous that I regularly fell asleep as soon as my head hit the pillow.

Added to the stress of being newly married while undertaking a ridiculous study workload, Sara and I headed up the church evangelism group. This started as a coffee and chat session in the old church buildings showing the Francis Schaeffer films *How Should We Then Live?*[16]

It wasn't that successful, so we moved up a gear and went witnessing at the Octagon on Friday nights. We all met for prayer and those who felt led to then went in twos down to the pits of Dunedin to talk to prostitutes, drunks and general troublemakers. We had made our own personal tracts about Jesus but also used some commercial ones.

At first, there was no obvious fruit, only opposition. One of our members was assaulted which resulted in him having headaches and dizzy spells for years. We broke up a few fights which gave us a good reputation with the police, but it was still very dangerous.

Then breakthrough came. We stumbled on a group of Māoris who had recently become Christians and were looking for a church to call home. They were a rough bunch who smoked a lot and had plenty of tattoos. We embraced them with open arms – not so the rest of our church, who were uncomfortable to say the least.

Eventually, the leader wanted to set a good example by being baptised. It was all arranged and about to happen when I discovered that he and his partner were not married but were openly in an active sexual relationship. I told the pastor who instructed me to call the baptism off. And that was the last we saw of them.

I wasn't too happy with the church or our leadership over that incident. To appease me, the pastor let me preach for the first time. The 'Old Testament Prophet' in me really came out and I let the church have it with a sermon crammed full of correction and condemnation. I was like a modern-day Moses throwing down the tablets of the Ten Commandments in disgust. For the first and only time I can remember, the church full of noisy Pentecostals was very quiet after that service.

Sara and I were young and bold, prone to outbursts and speaking our minds, but our hearts were wholehearted for God and we were certainly in love.

I am so glad that we got through that year and did not give up. Sara told me decades later that she used to lie awake at night thinking, 'How can I spend the rest of my life like this? It's all too hard.'

Love in a marriage is hard because it involves two imperfect people. But with a third perfect being in the relationship there is great hope and change.

Message to men (MTM)

Anyone with a modicum of personal insight knows that we are imperfect as people. In the marriage context, great lovers aren't born, they are made.

As men, where we can go wrong is to think that we are the ones who make straight that which is wonky. Our natural tendency is to think it's our spouse who needs to change, or at the very least to see things our way.

Put bluntly, it's not your job to 'fix her'. Your job is to love her, without strings attached, by getting your own act together.

When we boil it down, it's a matter of which way do you lean in your marriage? If you are leaning on your wife, making demands that she change and fiercely protecting your ways, then you will eventually topple. However, if you are leaning on God as the rock of all and allowing him to make the necessary adjustments in you, then you are in for the amazing journey of a lifetime.

The process of growth can be painful and humbling but, in the end, we move inch by inch, year by year from good to great.

Trust in the Lord with all your heart and lean not on
your own understanding; in all your ways submit to him,
and he will make your paths straight.
Proverbs 3:5-6

Chapter Thirteen
The Wonder of Science

World Events

- Springbok rugby tour of New Zealand divides the nation and incites widespread protests across the country
- Lady Diana Spencer and Charles the Prince of Wales marry
- The IBM PC signals the start of PCs at work and then into homes. In today's money, it would cost around $6,000 NZD for the first IBM PC
- I am exhausted having taken on too much trying to complete two degrees and my teacher training

Albert Einstein has been attributed as saying, 'The more I study science, the more I believe in God.[17]' This was certainly true for me as I studied psychology, botany, computer science and related topics. My faith stood firm in a God who by deliberate design created me and the wonderful universe I live in.

My world had considerably expanded with the advent of marriage. But at the end of our first year I was exhausted – it's astonishing how tiring it can be adjusting to life with another person and having to fight a nightly battle for your share of the blankets.

Sara was not quite so tired, having switched degrees from a science course that competed with medical students to a more sedate Bachelor of Arts. It was ironic that she was now doing a general degree available at any university in New Zealand.

That summer, I worked in Dunedin through the Student Job Scheme analysing the results of a huge psychology study. I had come to the attention of the Psych Department as a top student and as such, they were keen for me to do a Master's Degree.

I slaved away for hours carefully plotting the results of the investigation, only to arrive at the wrong conclusion in the eyes of the head researcher. He was convinced that the study would show a particular trend. Livid, he decided that I must have botched the analysis and set about 'doctoring' the results until he came up with what he wanted to see. So much for testing a theory through empirical evidence.

This was part of a rude awakening for me to the world of unscientific science. The following year, I took several papers on the History and Philosophy of Science.

I have never been so mentally stimulated as when we debated whether science was based on true fact, or whether it was akin to religion, or was indeed little more than philosophy by another name.

The current History of Science course starts with a bold quote that says, 'The past is a foreign country – they do things differently there.'[18] The Philosophy equivalent goes on to say, 'What is special about science? How are scientific theories generated? How are they tested? Can theories be conclusively established? What makes a good scientific explanation? To what extent is the succession of theories in the history of science driven by social forces?'[19]

There were three Christians in the group taking these papers. How do I know? It's because we were asked to identify ourselves during the first lecture within the first five minutes. Our role was to present the 'religious reasoning behind Christianity and science'. And I loved it.

Time and time again, we went through history looking at what was regarded as generally accepted and unquestionable fact. Then along came new thinkers (often Christians such as Copernicus, Galileo, Kepler, Newton and Boyle) who would challenge the body of common scientific knowledge. These men suffered incredible persecution at the hands of the establishment. Eventually, the new theory and associated evidence would win the hearts and minds of the scientific community, until it was challenged once more. And so, the cycle repeated itself.

I loved this stuff and actively participated. The final grade was based on just one assignment so I studied hard for it and read widely. I set about writing a paper clearly stating the case for Christianity as being more fact than fiction and how it was not incompatible with science. The lecturer was open-minded but as hard on Christians as he was on scientists. He firmly believed that both Christianity and science were totally based on assumption and blind faith and that real facts were few and far between.

To my delight I scored an A+. To my horror, the lecturer couldn't stop talking about my paper. He mentioned it during the last lecture and then, at the end of year party, he got drunk and proceeded to tell everyone who would listen about the details of what I had written. The Lord must have had a laugh as the gospel was being loudly proclaimed by an eccentric philosopher who was heavily under the influence.

These years in Dunedin were times of much discussion and debate with fellow students. Many were curious as to why we bothered getting married so young while still at university. There was no financial advantage to it or any other compelling reason in their eyes. This opened up many conversations where Sara and I would get to share the reasons behind our belief in an awesome God.

Despite all the shortcomings of university life, the students were at least open to learning. They weren't necessarily open-minded but there was an unwritten code that demanded respect for differing views, provided they were presented in a logical and well thought-out manner.

One time, the Christian group held a debate with students looking at some of the tough questions of life. After about an hour of answering a barrage of accusations-come-questions, one of the students remarked in a derogatory way, 'You Christians have it all summed up. You have answers for everything.' Nowadays I'm not as sure about that; many of the incredibly hard topics such as suffering and violence in the name of religion cannot be satisfactorily addressed by anyone but the Lord himself.

Our world in those early days was heavily focused on academia and Church. This was a good thing as our chief interests were well-aligned. Sara and I studied together for the end of semester exams.

We had an efficient system of increasing the hours of study over the weeks so we peaked at the right time. Our days were divided into three with one section completely free from study. During the other times we studied for an hour and then played cards together for ten minutes before resuming work. The day would be broken up for me by going for a run to clear the head and restart the learning process over again.

This was a good life lesson for us regarding encouragement, spurring each other on to greater things and holding each other accountable to commitments we had made. It also introduced the famous Carey Plans and Lists that have been the subject of much teasing over the years.

For me, the wonder of science was double-edged. It was fascinating as a subject. But it was also a weapon used by some to self-righteously assert that religion was for the weak-minded who couldn't stomach the real facts.

I suspected that at least one History and Philosophy professor that year was not so sure about that any more. Like me, countless scientists throughout the ages and many Nobel Prize winners[20] of more recent times saw no conflict between science and their faith in God.

Science can be equally harsh on the subject of love, telling us that falling in love can have neurological effects similar to those of cocaine. But love is more than some fickle emotion or temporary drug. It is an essential ingredient in what makes the world a better place.

I knew for certain that my wife loved me and I loved her. She certainly had made my world better.

Message to men (MTM)

Knowledge and wisdom are not the same thing. A simple person can have wisdom and experience incredible happiness whereas even a very smart person can do foolish things which leads to a destructive lifestyle.

In our society, we tend to hold in high regard those with much knowledge, often being in awe of their intelligence. For example, in social settings we defer to those who are outspoken and know the most about cars, or sport, or technology, or economics – in fact, any topic that we hold as important. But wisdom is a quiet thing that does not promote itself, often coming from a place where we consistently make good choices.

For Christians, this is one of those areas where we need a substantive shift in thinking. We have been conditioned to think that those who know the most are the top dogs. But in God's kingdom, it's more about insight and wisdom which comes from him.

Men, let's base our relationships on wisdom, not knowledge alone; in this there is true life and a better chance of happiness with our wives.

Cry out for insight, and ask for understanding. Search for them as you would for silver; seek them like hidden treasures. Then you will understand what it means to fear the Lord, and you will gain knowledge of God. For the Lord grants wisdom!
Proverbs 2:3-6, NLT

Chapter Fourteen
Friends Make the World Go Round

World Events

- Bob Marley dies from cancer aged thirty-six
- The first game of paintball is played in New Hampshire
- MTV is born as the first twenty-four-hour-a-day music television station
- We live in a community of Christians with around twenty-nine people from our church within a 100-metre radius of each other

It's an interesting thought that marriages started shifting from arranged-based to love-based only in the eighteenth century. Since the dawn of men and women, most marriages have started without all that lovestruck stuff we expect today. Your parents determined who you would wed, and you were expected to stay married to that person for your entire adult life.

Are modern marriages better than before? The statistics would indicate otherwise. Does being in love first really matter? Possibly, but since the essence of lasting love is choice, we can grow to truly love others, especially if other ingredients like respect and trust are present to sweeten the mix.

One thing that really helped Sara and me was good friends, and we had plenty. I sometimes look back on those years with envy, as our life in the suburbs can seem so isolated and insular in comparison.

Dunedin wasn't all study and work. We had loads of fun living in an area that collectively housed twenty-nine people from our church. Within this 100-metre radius there was an active community of believers. Together we shared meals, pooled our meagre resources (we didn't own a vacuum cleaner until we left Dunedin), counselled and comforted one another and, of course, had endless card games.

Our flat was strategically situated on the corner of a main street and the street that led to the university. Many a time we sat in our bay window watching the students going to and from lectures. Without fail, we would see someone we knew and with a beckoning wave, they would soon join us for a meal or a hot drink on those frosty Dunedin mornings.

One of the houses in our community was run by our best friends. Neil and Sandra were in their thirties and had twin two-year-olds, a girl and a boy. Theirs was an open home with three to four singles and usually another family living with them too.

It was nearly impossible to pass by without being drawn inside for coffee, a meal, or a chat. Often, we found a group sitting round the table engrossed in the latest card game. Their hospitality was legendary and became the model on which Sara and I based our own family life.

That winter, we went away on holiday with them (by bus as no one had a car) to the wonderful Central Otago with its many breathtaking lakes. But instead of fully appreciating the world-class scenery, Neil and I entered into the holiday spirit by playing endless games of chess. I was well outclassed intellectually by a man who is a genius, but he had a weakness – impatience, where he struggled to think too far ahead.

To his frustration, I would beat him almost every time by my plotting and scheming. The women were not too impressed by the men playing grown-up games when there were little toddlers who needed entertaining and many jobs to do.

In contrast to our student mates, we also had friends who seemed rich. Rex was working and owned a car. His wife, Jean, was at teachers' college with me. They were generous people and took us on several holidays. One time, we stayed at a Ministry of Work's cabin where we had to put money in a meter for the electricity. More than once it ran out and we stumbled around in the dark looking for coins and a torch.

That year saw much of the same regarding the evangelism group. The group had grown to more than twenty people, and by now we had made many lifelong friends. We continued to meet at our little flat, crammed into every available space, but this was a real sacrifice for us.

The hungry and thirsty team would return from the streets late at night to deplete our stocks of food and drink, leaving Sara in tears. We just couldn't afford to cater for so many and most of them were not in a position to contribute. But Sara and I have always been of a mind that all challenges have a solution, somehow, somewhere.

Tithing[21] had been an important part of our lives for years and we had found great freedom and joy in giving. Therefore, we started what we still call 'People Money'. A small portion of our

89

regular giving was put aside for others to serve them. At times, we gave above and beyond our regular amount but on other occasions, we used 'People Money' for those in need or where our normal resources could not cope.

Once again, we found new freedom in being generous, although we had very little ourselves. Our firm belief as a married couple is that our heavenly Father is amazingly generous towards people. His plan to rescue us and bring us into his family is astonishing to anyone who takes the time to think about it. But he is also generous in what he gives us in life.

From the outset, we wanted to be generous like our heavenly Dad. Our conviction was that everything belongs to him anyway, we are just the caretakers of a tiny piece of his stuff. Sara and I have always valued the idea of 'holding things lightly and people close'.

Regarding tithing, we are so glad we continued to do this when we had so little. When the big salaries came later in life, it was natural just to continue on. Over the years, we certainly experienced that the more you earn, the more you need. Getting the right perspective on finances when you do not have much helps you to avoid being enslaved by the mighty dollar when you have a lot.

During the Easter of our first year of marriage, some of our friendships were sorely tested. My ex-flatmate – the tough medical student – and his fiancé decided to do a tramp (hiking or backpacking) and invited a bunch of friends to join them.

Now, the Careys always like to be prepared. Having done plenty of tramping before, we planned this carefully, ensuring we had all the right gear and that our packs were not too heavy.

However, most of the group were newbies, as were the leaders. Mistakes were made from the beginning.

There was no inspection of the team's packs and no one outside the group was told where we were going. We then set off at a cracking pace. The leaders were ultra-fit and would steam off ahead until out of sight. We would then find them waiting for us, only to see them get up and move on again before we reached their spot. If we had rested, we would have lost them entirely.

The team of a dozen were mainly unfit and their packs were too heavy. When we finally arrived at the hut, we found that it was a shepherd's shelter approximately two metres by two metres with nothing but a dirt floor. I must admit that by now I was getting cross with our leaders, who seemed oblivious to the plight of the struggling group.

With the help of the others, I used my skills to build a bivouac out of branches from nearby trees. We built this against the hut with a fire by the entrance. I became quite pushy by this time because literally lives were at stake. The day had become cold and misty and the group was tired and hungry.

We then emptied all the unnecessary rubbish out of people's packs to find most of the sleeping bags were summer weight and not suitable for the climate we were in.

So needs must, we zipped together Sara's bag and mine (which were rated at twenty below zero) and three of us piled into it for the night. The extra sleeping bag was used by the person with the thinnest one as a double. Somehow, we got through the night by keeping the fire stoked and huddling together.

The next day, despite our discussion, the leaders set off at an extreme speed once more and we got lost. That's when rebellion set in. Half the group wanted to go back and the other half wanted to continue on. At least two of the group could no longer carry their packs and were in favour of just dumping them. Needless to say, there were tears, and angry words were exchanged. When we finally caught up with the leader, he did a remarkable thing by carrying two packs, one on his back and one on his front. The contents of the other pack were shared out among the others.

Our two most exhausted members no longer had packs to carry. But we were still lost and there were blisters, the mist and the cold to contend with. I was getting very concerned at this stage as they were showing early signs of hyperthermia.

Just when all seemed lost, we stumbled across a Land Rover parked on a track we had come to. Some of us waited by it while the others went on. Eventually the owner of the vehicle returned and immediately saw what a sorry state we were in.

As the Land Rover drove along the track, it picked up the various members of our team until we were half hanging out the doors and windows. After about an hour's drive we came across our leaders steadily plodding on, with three packs between them, still seemingly oblivious. We left them to finish the trek and drove back to civilisation and a hot bath.

My kids sometimes tease me about being Mr Safety or Mr Overprepared. But it is experiences like this which helped shape that character in me. Friends are great and they definitely enrich your life, but caution is needed when you put your family's safety and well-being in their hands.

Funnily enough, this is not too dissimilar to marriage. For it to thrive we need to make ourselves entirely vulnerable and to entrust our life into the care of another. This is something which is really difficult to be prepared for.

Message to men (MTM)

As enlightened men and fathers, we spend large amounts of time focusing on our relationships with spouses and blood relatives. But what about friends? It seems blokes aren't very good at making and maintaining close friendships. We often leave the 'social' side of things to our wives.

So, what happened to all those good friends from school and university, from sports teams, or our first jobs? Let's face it – we men tend to let friendships lapse. Work and family take a lot of our time and as a way of coping we end up drifting into social isolation.

A 2014 study[22] done in New Zealand showed that that well-connected people were less likely to experience illness, depression, or unemployment. The same study concluded that men had less numbers of close friends than women.

There is real power in asking each other, on a regular basis, things like, 'Are you OK?' or 'How is your relationship with God?' or 'Are things good between you and your wife?' And then doing a deeper dive into the answers.

Take a leaf out of our wives' book; connect well – you will then live well. That is why they outlast most of us.

Do not forsake your friend or a friend of your family …
Proverbs 27:10

Chapter Fifteen
School Days

World Events

- Michael Jackson's *Thriller* is the first album to sell 30 million albums and eventually becomes the largest selling record ever
- Argentina invades the Falklands but has to withdraw after two months
- The Commodore 64 home computer is launched. Three years later I created one of the first computer rooms in New Zealand schools by networking nine of these together
- Sara and I move to Wainuiomata in Wellington

Did you know that the Spanish word for wife, *esposas*, also means handcuff? There are at least two ways you can look at that; the positive is rather cool, implying that the two of you are connected in life by a great bond.

Our first two years of marriage had been hard, but our bond was stronger than ever. Being married was like holding a mirror up to myself, where I saw all my selfishness and foibles for the first time.

I had finished two degrees and teachers' college training by the skin of my teeth. This saying is actually from the book of Job, chapter 19 and verse 20, where he describes himself as having escaped death by the skin of his teeth. I felt the same after such an exhausting and trying year.

Sara and I decided that five years for me at university was enough and that putting patches on patches on the knees of our jeans was a step too far. Hence, I opted to journey from the world of the great unwashed to the life of a working man.

As a first-year teacher, I was required to designate my preferred region in New Zealand and at what level I wanted to teach. Naturally, I put Dunedin as my first choice as we loved living there and had such a great Christian community around us. I also indicated that I wanted to teach five to six-year-olds.

In 1982 it was rare for a man to teach juniors, but I knew that was where my heart was. Lesley, my mother-in-law, had shown me that young kids were pure sponges of learning. I got my wish but not in the city we had hoped for.

My one-year appointment was at a school in Wainuiomata, close to Wellington. That was good and bad. Good that we were near Sara's parents (who had returned to Wellington) and bad in that Wainuiomata was not a desirable place to be.

Wainui, as it is known, was also called Nappy Valley; a small isolated community only accessible by a steep hill road. Its nickname came about when hundreds of families flocked there in the 1950s due to the availability of affordable housing. With so many impoverished people in one spot it soon became a working-class area that was shut off from the rest of Wellington by a very imposing hill. The community bred tough kids, as I was about to find out.

Sara was gutted about us living and me working in Wainui. She came to New Zealand from England when she was four and had grown up in a nice suburb with wonderful views across the harbour. Nappy Valley was the last place she ever thought she would end up.

Wainui proved a shock to us, but I also proved a shock to the school. On my first day, I pulled into the car park in a Mini. Everyone was watching to see who the new teachers would be, when out of this tiny car unpeeled a six-foot-two bearded giant. I still remember the gasps of the children as they looked on in surprise.

My class was also stunned by the appearance of a man. One little girl was so frightened that she climbed under her desk and refused to come out. It was then I decided I needed to do something about my Old Testament appearance and try to become a little less scary.

Nobody could figure out why a man with two degrees wanted to teach little ones. The headmaster thought it was ridiculous and took every opportunity to tell me I was wasted babysitting juniors. I, of course, stood my ground and he took an instant dislike to me. Once again, I managed to make a bad start in a new situation.

Even the kids struggled with the concept of a male teacher. One morning that same little girl plucked up the courage to ask, 'Mr Carey, don't you go to work?' I explained that teaching was my job, but still the children remained mystified by me.

A bit later, another child arrived early and saw that I was at school, having still been there when she had left at the end of the previous day. Confused, she asked, 'Mr Carey, do you live at the school? Don't you have a home?'

It certainly felt that way as a first-year teacher. Every waking moment was spent preparing for the next day. It was like I was stuck on a hamster wheel and couldn't get off. Thank God for my supportive wife who spent many hours helping me make teaching resources that the school couldn't afford. Lesley was also full of useful advice whenever I was stuck for ideas or facing new issues.

Life was a bit easier for Sara as she had a further two years of study to go. However, without me to spur her on she found university really difficult.

Despite my initial setbacks, I had a wonderful year with the children. They were indeed sponges and soaked up everything I taught them. The atmosphere in the classroom was one of fun and curiosity. My three fellow junior teachers, all female, soon took me under their wing and were amazingly supportive. They were experienced teachers and very matter of fact with the children, as I soon discovered.

Our first trip to the swimming pool as a syndicate is forever imprinted in my mind. Being new, I just followed suit as the teachers lined the kids up alongside the pool and told them to get undressed and into their swimsuits. I was horrified that we weren't using the changing rooms and I am sure I went bright red with embarrassment. But the children obliged with only mild protests. Just when it seemed too much, light relief came when I noticed the five-year-old girls all standing together covering their bare chests with their hands to stop the boys from peaking at their nonexistent breasts.

I am sure there would be a local outcry (if not world headlines) if we put children through that sort of thing today. But as I said earlier, these children were tough and didn't get fazed by such things.

There were problems, however, that were more serious. Several of the children were neglected. They would brag that they were allowed to stay up past midnight during the week watching inappropriate adult movies with their siblings. It was not uncommon for some to fall asleep in my classroom after lunch.

A number of the children had hygiene problems and I was often ringing the health nurse for assistance. Mostly alarming of all was that quite a few were not eating properly. The Parent Teacher Association decided to provide free lunches based on the knowledge that children cannot learn if they are hungry. It was a good intention, but harder to put into practice than you might think. The children were so used to eating bad food that the only free lunch they would willingly eat was marmite and chippie (crisps) sandwiches.

I got through the year, having thoroughly enjoyed the kids and the teaching but not the staff politics. The headmaster and I avoided each other, but I did find out that he was opposed to me being formally certified as a fully fledged teacher. The senior teacher of the junior school was livid and spoke her mind to him. The whole school heard about it.

Fortunately, this teaching appointment was for just one year. At the school Christmas function, the other first-year teacher received a big bunch of flowers from the headmaster along with a lovely gift. Since I had been made responsible for science in the school, I was ungraciously given a second-hand test tube with a school biro in it as my farewell present. My boss was more than livid this time. One by one the other teachers came to me to apologise for the headmaster's behaviour.

To be honest, I was perplexed. It seemed that I was friendly with most people, but in my working life spanning thirty-seven years, there has always seemed to be one person who took a dislike to me. Without fail they were bullies, my stereotypical nemesis. I guess, like esposas being Spanish for wife and handcuff, I had a choice to treat these people as a positive or a negative thing in my life. Many times when I have looked back, I have taken the destructive route of holding a grudge against bullies only to eventually repent and forgive them. In the meantime, I have allowed their behaviour to rob me of real joy and cause me untold stress.

Lord, give me wisdom to know when I am handcuffed to a set of behaviours that undermines relationships, especially in my marriage.

Message to men (MTM)

Do men have more destructive tendencies than women? It depends how you look at it, but it is difficult to deny that many of our behaviours are more harmful.

Men tend to be more successful at suicide than woman by a factor of more than three. More men die behind the wheel of a car at a similar ratio. They are twice as likely as women to be alcoholics and three times more likely to be drug addicts. Men are eight times (at least) more likely to end up in prison than women. Not surprisingly, women outlive men – in New Zealand by around four years.[23]

It has been said that men are moths to the flame of risky behaviour. If we want our marriages to flourish and as a consequence, our families also, we need to examine ourselves periodically regarding what pushes our self-destruct buttons.

As men, we all have them – these tendencies to take silly risks or do things that are harmful. Mine was anger and resentment against bullies who seemed to plague my life. What are yours?

There is a [behaviour] that appears to be right, but in the end it leads to death.
Proverbs 14:12

Chapter Sixteen
A Summer to Remember

World Events

- The musical Cats opens on Broadway and becomes Broadway's longest-running play
- A permanent artificial heart is implanted in a human for first time
- It costs just over $3 to go to the movies in New Zealand
- Sara and I buy a house in Wainuiomata despite being students for five years and calculating it would take fifteen years to save for a deposit

Some summers stick in your mind like a permanent feature. I have lived through 241 seasons but this summer was certainly one to remember.

In the time before I started work as a teacher, we stayed with Pop and Lesley at their place in Island Bay, a suburb in Wellington. Yet again, they had been amazingly generous to us by lending us money for a car and then refusing any repayments. They had a knack of doing this just when we were desperate, and it made such a difference to our lives.

Over the years, we have tried to model this with our own children – being generous but not doing so much that they can't stand on their own two feet.

That summer was hard. I knew Pop had an acute dislike for me and I tried my best to earn his favour. In the end, it took seven years before we became true friends – a bit like the story of Jacob and the seven years he worked for Rachel his wife, found in Genesis 29.

Pop was busy building a garage with a sleep-out as an extension to their tiny home. To help, I dug out masses of sticky clay for the foundations and carted many wheelbarrows of builders' mix down the very steep driveway. It was back-breaking work. Like Jacob, I was basically a slave to my father-in-law, but to no avail. By the end of the summer I was tired and miserable.

To make matters worse, living with Sara's parents created a new set of tensions for us that we had not anticipated. Sara reverted to being 'Sara Harrison' and while she was in their home I was pushed into the background. Sara let her parents' influence dominate. The 'favourite and only daughter' had come home but my wife had ceased to exist.

It wasn't until decades later that we discovered this is fairly typical behaviour which occurs as couples work through what it means to leave their parents and cleave to each other, as we read in the Bible, in Genesis 2:24. A new family nucleus is being formed where decision-making and focus shifts to the marriage instead of relying on the parents.

Very quickly I became desperate to leave Island Bay and to start our life together in Wainuiomata. Sara and I looked at the finances and they looked back at us with grim faces. I have not been completely honest when I said we were poor; when I sold my Mark III Cortina the money was squirrelled away and largely forgotten about. But even that was small change in the great scheme of things.

Although Sara is a master at bookkeeping, I was always the one who pushed the financial boundaries in our marriage. I wanted to know for sure what options we had, so Sara set about calculating and found that it would take fifteen years to afford our first home. Our hearts sank as we realised the only real option was to rent again.

Just when we had given up in the face of overwhelming data, we saw an advertisement that said, 'Why rent when you can buy?' Intrigued, we investigated it further and to our surprise found it was indeed possible.

Our heavenly Father decided that he would align a bunch of disconnected factors to make this happen. Firstly, houses in Wainui were dirt cheap. That massive hill had kept prices down to about a quarter of those in adjacent areas. This meant that our 'squirrelled' savings were just enough for a deposit. The government had a special grant and tax exemption for first-time home owners which made it affordable on my teacher's wage. This lasted only a year and we came in at the tail end, just before it wound up. Interest rates were reasonably low and the banks were uncharacteristically keen to help young first-time home owners.

This is the type of miracle that we need to recall when we begin to doubt that God is truly a provider who loves to be generous. There was no way in this universe we could have expected to have our own home by the end of that summer. It was a faith-stretch too far. But our expectations were far exceeded by a God who is good and who has marvellous plans for us.

All a dither with excitement, we contacted a Wainui real estate agent. He turned out to be a Christian who went to our future church. Don gave us incredibly honest and helpful advice, forever blowing away the myth that all real estate agents are rogues and robbers.

We looked at townhouse after townhouse until they began to blur into one. My saving grace was that I took notes. Sara reached the point of overload and said to me, 'Just pick one, any one and I promise I will be happy.' So, I did, but she wasn't.

When I took her to see it, the curtains were drawn, the place was stuffed with oversized furniture and the lady was cooking tripe. When we stepped outside, I excitedly said, 'What do you think?' My poor wife didn't say anything, she just cried.

The place turned out to be wonderful. It was slightly bigger than most townhouses and the location was in one of the best areas in Wainuiomata. With a bit of elbow grease and lots of handyman effort, we transformed it.

Pop had been buying me tools as birthday and Christmas presents, so we set about wallpapering, painting the outside of the house, putting up curtains, tiling the kitchen and building a pantry.

My pride and joy was the fence I built. Within weeks of completing it, a neighbour skidded off the road on his motorbike and crashed through it. I was genuinely upset that my work of art had been defaced. He said he would fix it and he did, supplying me with a dozen beers along the way to calm my angst.

I was to build a number of fences over the years, all of which were masterpieces in my mind. To my horror, every single one of them was demolished by the new owners once they moved in. I still don't understand why!

Our wee townhouse was a happy place and it felt very much 'us' once we had decorated it to suit our personalities. I still feel a tingle down my spine when I think how impossible it was for us ever to have bought it – from poor students to homeowners in the space of a few months.

Everything about it was so right. The cost of the mortgage was in fact $3 a week less than we had been paying for rent in Dunedin. We sold the townhouse two and half years later for over twice what we had paid for it. Thirty years on and those properties have barely doubled again in price. It would seem that timing was everything, subject to a God who got it so right for us.

It was truly a summer to remember for many reasons. Most importantly it reminds us of God's great blessing in getting us started on the property ladder fifteen years ahead of schedule.

Message to men (MTM)

I have heard it said that money is a game. In a marriage the only way to win that game is to be on the same team.

How do you achieve this when so often one of you is a spender and the other a saver, when money consistently tops the list as the number one cause of breakdowns between couples, and when financial secrets in relationships are commonplace?

Toxic financial habits and attitudes are very destructive in a marriage. As a Christian and a man, one of those toxic beliefs is to think that providing for our family is our responsibility. This can drive us to work long hours or to be stingy with money, or become judgemental, especially of our wives, when they seem to have so many financial wants.

One thing our Lord has repeatedly taught me at various times during my life is that God alone is our provider. He is the Father of all and his heart towards me is amazingly generous. We do our bit but we don't have to sweat it or drive ourselves into an early grave trying foolishly to enrich our lives.

Do not wear yourself out to get rich; do not trust your own cleverness. Cast but a glance at riches, and they are gone, for they will surely sprout wings and fly off to the sky like an eagle.
Proverbs 23:4-5

Chapter Seventeen
A Church Full of Cars

World Events

- *Time* magazine 'Man of the Year' is the computer
- Motorola introduces the first mobile phones to the USA
- Microsoft releases 'Word', their word processing program
- The NZD $50 note is added
- I am struggling with the workload of being a new teacher and coping with the demands of church life

A long time ago I heard a saying by the preacher Billy Sunday that went: 'Going to church doesn't make you a Christian any more than going to a garage makes you an automobile.'[24] That tickled my fancy but I also knew it had a serious side to it. Churches aren't perfect by any stretch of the imagination – they are full of people. Yet without a church family around us our faith grows cold, like a hot ember that dies when taken from the blazing fire.

In our marriage, our love for God was central. It was the hub by which everything else revolved. In fact, Sara and I believe that our marriage is a threesome, in a spiritual sense, where the Lord is the source of our wisdom and strength.

Finding a church that summer was not much of an issue since there weren't many to choose from in small town Wainuiomata, but we wanted to find more than a building, or a social club of likeminded people. We wanted a place that would become our spiritual home, where people were alive to things of God and cared for others.

A.W. Tozer explained it like this, 'One hundred religious persons knit into a unity by careful organization do not constitute a church any more than eleven dead men make a football team. The first requisite is life, always.'[25]

So, we found the local Baptist church. Since the pastor had recently come from Dunedin we figured he must be a good guy (it's amazing how one-eyed we had become about Dunedin in a short period of time).

Apparently, the whole church was abuzz about these two university-educated young people joining them. It was a bit intimidating for them and us until they discovered we were ordinary folk who loved God.

Nonetheless, we were quickly to discover the church had its share of challenges. Tensions over the Holy Spirit were forefront, as was common back then. We had largely forgotten about that, having attended a Pentecostal church for the last three years – so it was a shock to us all over again.

The powerbase in the church was a few well-established families. Being a democratically run domination, their sway was enormous. Don't get me wrong, I have nothing against democracy. It has its place, but not in Christianity – God alone is the head. After all, for God so loved the world that he didn't send a committee.

The worst thing about the church was that there was so little understanding about the meaning of grace. Sara and I understood grace more by intuition than theology, as we had never had any solid teaching on it. Most of what we had heard was do more, try harder, pray longer and study your Bible unceasingly. The churches that we knew tended to reflect the work ethic of Western society where reward was directly proportional to the effort put in. While this is fine to a degree, it is not the message of the gospel. The Christian author Philip Yancey summed up grace like this: 'There is nothing you can do to make God love you more. There is nothing you can do to make God love you less.'[26] Grace is about God's undeserved love towards us. His love is not earned, nor is his favour coloured by whether we are good people. God loves us regardless.

Despite it being at the heart of the message Jesus brought to earth, Sara and I did not hear teaching like this until we went to England decades later. In the meantime, we were part of a church of people who were incredibly driven.

Everything about my Christian life felt like it was not enough. The answer to life was outwardly proclaimed as being Jesus, but beneath the surface it was about doing more and being a better person.

The expectations on Sara and me were outrageous and we found it exhausting. The church met twice on a Sunday and it was noted if you were not there for both services. We quickly got involved in running a young persons' small group at our home. We were part of almost everything going. But with Sara's study and my workload as a new teacher it was a crippling load on our already burdened backs.

It was during this period of our marriage that we developed our philosophy that when we say yes to people, we really mean it. Conversely, when we say no, it is with sincerity – no games played.

At first people didn't like it and some were offended by the bluntness of it. But those who cared about us soon realised that our honesty was worth more than our reluctant compliance, as they got our full and undivided involvement.

However, it was not smooth sailing. We wanted to support the pastor in his struggles to see the church come alive and grow, but we couldn't always satisfy his demands on us as a 'key couple'. When Easter came around that year, it was expected that we would go to the youth camp and help lead it. Instead, we did a biblical Jonah and ran in the opposite direction, camping at Castlepoint. Why we chose a remote, windswept beach miles from anywhere is as crazy as Jonah's choice to go to Tarshish.

We huddled together in our tent using our sleeping bags for warmth, trying to read our books by torchlight in the semi-darkness of a storm. The wind became so fierce that our tent started to rip. At that moment we realised how foolish we had been and repented. We asked God for forgiveness as we packed up our tent in the wind and the rain and drove home feeling thoroughly sorry for ourselves. At least, there was no great fish in the story – just a storm and fearing for our lives.

We were incredibly tired and hardly found any times for genuine relaxation. Life seemed to consist of working or being at church with the fun bits in-between missing.

We needed to rest each week, which funnily enough is what God instructed us to do at the very beginning of his creation. He said that for one day a week you must remove yourself from work and all stressful activities so you can just chill.

The Lord himself set the example by walking in the cool of the evening in the garden with Adam and Eve (see Genesis 3:8). In our ultra-busy lives, we easily forget how to take a stroll with God and just commune with him and each other.

The result is stress, not rest. Unfortunately, many people in our culture wear stress and busyness as a badge of honour. Danzae Pace said: 'Stress is the trash of modern life – we all generate it but if you don't dispose of it properly, it will pile up and overtake your life.'[27]

It was certainly piling up in our lives that year. In fact, for many years it continued to heap on me until I became victim to its poison – but that's another story for another book.

On the upside, the church had some really great people. Our small group was full of radicals who wanted to make a difference. Pat and Janette were ten years our senior and the leaders of our group. They helped us get established in Wainui and provided much-needed muscle power and advice with the decorating. We loved our long quirky discussions with this couple over what Christianity and Church were really about.

Michelle and Nicholas were also nonconformists. They were young Christians who eventually became lifelong friends. Our children and theirs grew up like brothers and sisters, for reasons I will explain later.

Due to the pressures of that year it was tempting to compartmentalise Christianity to a few meetings during the week and two on a Sunday. But we were not like that. Both Sara and I were determined to be wholehearted in our journey towards God.

Jesus had set me free from so much and now the church was my new family – warts and all. My heavenly Father had adopted me as his son (see Romans 8:15-17) and he wanted full custody, not just weekend visits.

Message to men (MTM)

I love the saying 'we are in lockstep'. It implies marching in the same direction, legs moving in perfect timing with each other. This should be our goal both in marriage and in our relationship with our heavenly Father.

Restricting our faith to certain actions or weekly events is not lockstep but a poor imitation. Lockstep implies being in sync, in tune, with a depth of oneness that can only come from moving the same way.

Men, what our families and our marriages need most is for us to be on fire for God – to become white hot worshippers of him and to know him and his ways intimately. When we live a daily life of hearing from the Holy Spirit we become in lockstep, and only then we can begin to transform our marriages in the same way.

We have a Father who loves us beyond all else. His desire is for us to be one with him. As lockstep implies, he wants full custody, and not just on Sundays.

The Lord directs our steps, so why try to understand
everything along the way?
Proverbs 20:24, NLT

Chapter Eighteen
The Money Go Round

World Events

- Apple Macintosh computers hits the market with a storm
- United States researchers discover the AIDS virus
- Tetris is officially released in the Soviet Union
- Sara and I are DINKYs – Dual Income, No Kids Yet

In his day John D. Rockefeller was one of the richest men in the world. For all practical purposes, his money was virtually limitless. Someone supposedly asked him, 'How much money is enough money?' Rockefeller is said to have replied, 'Just a little bit more.'[28]

Almost overnight being poor became a dim memory for us. As homeowners with a steady income, life was looking up. In 1984 Sara began teaching and we were labelled DINKY – Dual Income, No Kids Yet. Even so we weren't stereotypical as we resisted selling our souls to the god of credit cards.

New Zealand in the 1980s saw deregulation that allowed high interest rates and penalty fees on credit cards, which allegedly meant they became a major source of profit for banks. The use of credit cards exploded and scores of young couples like us were soon buried under an avalanche of credit card debt. Many maxed out their credit cards and were taking on new ones just to pay off the astronomical interest payments, thus becoming entrapped in a cycle of debt.

We were spared that, but for the first time we began to have quarrels over money. With our needs skyrocketing through having a house, a car and jobs we discovered that we had embarked upon marriage with very different attitudes towards money.

This was new ground for us and it took our disagreements to another level – in marriage it seems the learning never stops. There are always dangers and benefits to arguing. Care is needed if you are determined to win an argument at all costs, especially when it concerns what you buy.

This story perfectly illustrates this point. The elderly father of a very good friend of ours decided one day that he would do his own clothes shopping for a change. After a stint at a men's shop he proudly walked into the house wearing a beautiful checked shirt.

His wife's reaction was to scold him for wearing clothes that were twenty years too young for a man in his seventies and she told him to take it back immediately. She stated emphatically that he should leave clothes shopping and fashion to her and that he should stick with what he knows best.

After an unpleasant exchange of words, he marched out of the door and back to the shop. He returned a couple of hours later towing an enormous boat behind the car. She apparently never said a word.

Sara and I were never that extreme, but nevertheless we had other issues.

Giving came naturally to both of us and our marriage was grounded on giving and being generous. Tithing was an integral part of who we were as it was for Rockefeller, who tithed 10 per cent of his earnings to his church starting with his very first pay cheque.

We lived by the principles aptly expressed by Clint Jr. Murchison who said, 'Money is like manure. If you spread it around it does a lot of good. But if you pile it up in one place it stinks like hell.'[29]

Where we were planets apart was with spending and saving. For a while we viewed each other's attitude towards money as alien and scary.

Sara preferred to stockpile and have reserves. I saw little sense in that approach when we needed so many things.

My tendencies were probably a reaction to growing up in an impoverished working-class family; hers was a more frugal approach typical of progressive middle-class immigrants.

My financial DNA played itself out through a tendency to be overly generous and to find it easy to spend money, especially on others. Christmas and birthdays saw their share of animated discussions as I often wanted to buy loads of presents whereas Sara was content to stop sooner than me.

As a male, I am unusual in that I like to shop. Sara, on the other hand, hates it. She is the only woman I know who is hard to spoil and she seldom spends money on herself. My wife is actually not that interested in clothes, or jewellery or the usual girlie things. Her Achilles' heel is shoes.

During one of our more recent 'discussions' over my obsession with buying DVD movies, I pointed out that she had hundreds of shoes. She scoffed at this so I opened her wardrobe to reveal several shelves of them. Having made my point, I noticed she went very quiet.

That's when I saw a large box sitting on the cupboard floor. A quick 'What's in the box?' from me drew a swift 'Nothing much' from her. Despite her protests I opened the box to find it bulging with shoes.

To give her credit, Sara was more into quality and I was fooled in those early days with the allure of quantity. Later, when I worked for Foreign Affairs and Trade and travelled a lot, I would often bring back a suitcase full of presents for the kids. I loved the looks on their faces as we sat on the lounge floor and opened each one. Despite years of advice from my wise wife, I persisted in buying as many cheap toys as I could, only to see them break in the first days of rough handling by overenthusiastic children.

I had also been duped into thinking that creating romance meant giving presents. Not so for Sara. We had many a cross word when I would buy her stuff as a romantic gesture that we couldn't really afford. Gifts are not her love language (more on that later) and so what I foolishly thought was a token of my love earned me a response I didn't expect.

All these financial foibles were hidden from each other when we first got married. As students, we had $20 a week for food and little else. There were few disagreements over money as we simply didn't have any to argue over. Once we started earning, things changed and we had more than a few battles.

It all quietened down when we agreed on an unusual thing called a budget. Motivational speaker and writer John C. Maxwell laid bare this mystery when he said, 'A budget is telling your money where to go instead of wondering where it went.'[30]

We adopted an approach known as Grandma's Jars. This was based on the old days, when everything was done with cash.

> Grandma used to have a row of jars on the mantelpiece – one for rent, one for food, one for power and so on. Each payday, the housekeeping money was divided up between the jars so that there [was] always enough to cover the bills and, with a bit of luck, some to set aside for a rainy day. The key to keeping control of your money is to use different accounts to manage each of [the] spending and saving categories, just like Grandma's jars on the mantelpiece.[31]

Sara's strength was in handling the accounts and doing a monthly snapshot of our finances using virtual jars. Occasionally we would sit down together and look at how things were going in each account, but I was better at looking at the big picture and ensuring we had some longer-term investments.

To help cope with our differences over the little things, we now run a simple pocket money system which we do not have to account to each other over. In more recent times, mine has mainly been for buying DVDs and Sara's, her 'rainy day and shoe fund'. It's a simple solution to what had been a big issue. Conflict over our incidental spending became a thing of the past.

But that didn't stop me from the occasional naughty acquisition. One particular time, we received a large tax return. If you recall, our year apart had conditioned me to be obsessed with clearing the letterbox. This day, I found the cheque from the Inland Revenue and hid it from Sara. Back then we still relied on cash so I also squirrelled away other money until I had enough to surprise my wife.

On Sara's birthday, I had a set of beautiful bedroom furniture delivered to replace our second-hand, rumpity drawers. She was both delighted and shocked. The ruse was so successful that my reputation as 'Honest Lon' was tainted in the mind of my unsuspecting and trusting wife.

Our income has grown exponentially over the years, but like Rockefeller, there is always a need for a little more. Doubling the wage doesn't double the disposable income or necessarily increase happiness and freedom. To Sara and me, we are well-off when we can be generous; but we are rich when money is our willing servant, not our cruel master. It has little to do with the fortune we possess. And yet as Mark Twain shrewdly said, 'I am opposed to millionaires, but it would be dangerous to offer me the position.'[32]

Many years later, the strength of our financial union would be seriously tested when we found ourselves swimming in debt while I was seriously ill, not knowing when I could work again. But that is decades away and there was plenty of growing up to do in the meantime.

Message to men (MTM)

Gifts bought lovingly are great, but the kind that are free often have the greatest impact. One of the best gifts you can give someone is encouragement.

It never ceases to amaze me that no matter how often I praise my grandkids, they lap it up. In fact, they will intentionally seek it if I am a bit slow to acknowledge their latest awe-inspiring feat.

As men we can be tight-fisted when it comes to gifting encouragement. Somehow deep in the recess of our macho brains we think praise makes people soft. There is some crazy belief locked away in there that reckons positive speak is for sissies.

On the other hand, criticism can roll off our male tongues without thought or effort. Criticism has its place when used wisely and sparingly, but it also has its dangers. The sad fact is that people, especially those close to us, tend to weigh negativity considerably more than positivity. And there is so much that is destructive in our world today that it has become the norm to bombard others with it.

For relationships to grow, the focus needs to be about creating the right conditions for people to flourish through genuine, sustained and deliberately applied encouragement. And what a gift that is! So be bold and generous with your gifts, especially your praise. Then witness the difference it makes to your relationship.

Words kill, words give life;
they're either poison or fruit – you choose.
Proverbs 18:21, *The Message*

Chapter Nineteen
Adversity

World Events

- Coca-Cola changes its formula and releases New Coke, which is a disaster
- The first mobile phone call is made in the UK
- NZ becomes nuclear free and refuses entry to the warship USS *Buchanan*
- I have a back accident that puts me in hospital for weeks

Out of adversity comes mastery. We learn to be resilient in our beliefs and discover strength and ability when it hurts. I am told that if you cut a butterfly out of its cocoon when it is ready to emerge, it will die. The butterfly needs to fight its way out to develop the muscle to live outside its protective shell.

Sara and I had big plans; actually, four of us had big plans – including Michelle and Nicholas. As we grew closer as couples, we began to open up to each other. We talked long about the concept of a Christianity that wasn't bound by materialism and crippled by the culture that threatened to swamp it. Topics like the poor and helping others were thrown in the mix to stir our hearts.

Over time, the idea grew wings and we decided to establish a Christian community, where we would share resources and free people's time to focus on others. After all, we figured, why do two families need two lawnmowers, or two washing machines, or two of any appliance? Living simply would enable two households to need less and create time to do God's work.

The idea strengthened each time we met, which was almost daily. Before long we had drawn up the plans for a house with three areas – one for them, one for us and one common area where others could live too. Then the snowball effect took over. Before we knew it, we had bought a plot of land together just outside Wainui. It was big enough to sustain four houses and had a lovely stream running through it in which I swear I saw trout.

After some investigation, we found an affordable house that came as a kit-set. They supplied a builder and I was to be the labourer during my summer holidays. The whole thing was like a giant wooden three-dimensional jigsaw. Things were looking good and all four of us got very excited – then disaster struck.

During one of our many church activities, I was helping clear an area for the church to use as parking. While carrying a heavy concrete block, one of the impetuous young helpers pressed down on it as a joke, asking if it was heavy. My back went click – something popped and I ended up in agony.

At first, Sara found it very difficult to get help. I was confined to the floor in our lounge. Any movement, such as crawling on all-fours to go to the toilet, ended in me being violently sick, which only made matters worse. Eventually, the local doctor came. He was grumpy about being called out so he took Sara aside and asked if I was a hypochondriac.

Needless to say, she was livid; we fired him and took on a doctor who was new to the area. He was not only very professional, but he became our friend. Sara and his wife still meet up occasionally and exchange notes on the kids and grandkids.

Dr Hans admitted me to hospital where I stayed for weeks on end. I was too young for surgery so they put me in traction to stretch my spine and bring some relief to the compacted discs. All thoughts of building were off, and incredibly we managed to halt the delivery of the materials just in time.

It was a hard season for me, wondering what this meant in my life. Our dream was shattered. But was I able to continue working as teacher, where I needed to be on my feet all day? And what about having children; would I ever be capable of active love-making again? All day long I just lay there in traction with thoughts going round and round in my head until I felt I was spinning out of control.

Eventually I had a meltdown, and the hospital had to bring Sara in to calm me. I was deeply worried and depressed, with emotions accentuated by the strong painkillers I was prescribed.

All through this time Sara never faltered. She remained upbeat and positive, believing that God had a purpose and that we would look back and see his handiwork even in this time of seeming disaster.

My lovely wife took the 'for better, for worse' vow to heart and was the strong one when I was weak and full of doubts. This happened time and time again in our marriage, where one of us was able to help the other get back on their feet when problems piled up on top of them.

Things began to change for the better. There is an old Chinese proverb that goes, 'I was sad because I had no shoes, until I met a man who had no feet.'

Once I took my eyes off my own condition, I saw that my ward was full of people worse off than me. Several had been in hospital for more than six months with chronic back problems and the prognosis was that they would never work again. One seventeen-year-old was admitted with advanced cancer. His life had been full of sorrow with an unhappy forced marriage due to an unplanned pregnancy. I got to share the gospel of hope with him and later went to the hospice to pray with him before he died.

There were lighter moments too when a roofer was placed in the bed next to me, having stapled his knee to his leg using a new-fangled thing called a nail gun. They had to operate to unhinge him so he could walk again. He took it all in good humour and discharged himself the next day.

I was out of action for around fourteen weeks while the traction slowly did its magic. Once home from hospital, I took over Michelle and Nicholas' lounge floor. Sara had already shifted in with them and we had begun the process of selling our townhouse. I lay on the floor week after week, and like the butterfly, I slowly gained the strength to fly.

Many people in the church came to see me and prayed for me. Although we saw no instant healing, I loved them doing that. Prayer to me is like phoning home. It was honouring to God and to me. I know my Lord does heal, it's in his DNA.

While I was lying about, the rest of the gang together bought a three-bedroom house in the nearby suburb of Petone. It didn't fit any of our requirements for community living. The idea was that we would completely renovate it and with the profits start again, this time getting someone else to do the building.

Before all this happened, I had taught in the Middle School at Upper Hutt for two years. It was my dream job, with a wonderful, older staff who were very supportive. Believe it or not, the headmaster thought I was great. He really encouraged me to pioneer computer education for seven to ten-year-olds. It was exciting and groundbreaking – the whole local community was abuzz about it. Just to keep me on my toes I also ran the chess club, produced a weekly class magazine and coached cricket, soccer and cross country. It was full-on fun with loads of intrinsic reward. But it was only a two-year tenure and sadly, I had to move on.

Before we got heavily into daydreaming with Michelle and Nicholas, Sara and I had decided to apply throughout the country for junior school teaching positions. We put our names forward for many country schools, completing well over 100 applications. There was only one school we applied for that was not at the junior level and yup, that's the one I got.

The school was an Intermediate in Lower Hutt built especially for eleven to thirteen-year-olds. I still think this is a weird New Zealand concept. It's the stage of life when girls hit puberty before boys and are actually bigger than them in most cases. I hated the constant squabbling and bickering among the hormonal teenage girls. I longed to be teaching little ones again and so over time lost my love for teaching and got thoroughly fed-up with the hard work.

Until my back accident the school had not been very supportive and the politics were unbearable. But all that seemed to change when I returned to work. They took the problem of a country-wide shortage of woodwork teachers and turned it into an opportunity for me to fill the vacancy as a full-time computer teacher, thinking it would be a long time before a new woodwork teacher could be found. Back in 1985 this was a very radical idea.

One of the 'mastery' things that came out of my back saga was my shifting interest to computing. I had already begun to get a bit of a reputation in the field of educational software. There were a small number of dedicated teachers who were creating free software for the public domain and I was one of them.

Many night hours were clocked up developing software for kids. I was also advising other schools and helping them set up their own computers. In 1985 this was radical. The district inspector got wind of this and after a word with my new headmaster, it was agreed to trial having me as a computer specialist in an Intermediate school.

Once I was fit for work again, I got an ergonomic chair that could be raised very high so I didn't have to stand all day. Using the sure-fire method of beg, steal or borrow, I obtained nine Commodore 64 computers and networked them to a single floppy drive. I had to pre-load everything an hour before class just to make sure it was ready in time.

Things went well for a term. Then more disaster struck. The school got a woodwork teacher so were forced to close me down. Rather than return to a class full of troubled teens, I quit.

It was Easter, so I picked up the phone and worked my way through my contacts in computer companies until I found one who was home. On the spot, I got a job which increased my salary and halved my pressure overnight. Or so I thought.

From adversity came change for the better. I had fought my way out of the cocoon of teaching and was now flying as a completely different creature in the field of computing. However, unlike butterflies which only live for a few days, I had morphed into this state for the next three decades.

Message to men (MTM)

When you think about the wimpiest man in history, who comes to mind? To me it's got to be Adam. He let his wife manipulate him into eating the forbidden fruit despite being explicitly told not to by the Lord. Then when he was caught out, he tried to act innocent and blame her for his behaviour.[33]

And so, Adam started an enduring trend which has seen generations of men exchange wisdom and faithfulness for instant pleasure.

So why did God allow this temptation? I believe it was so that men would learn to love him and trust him through the hard times and not just when they are prancing about in paradise, living the good life.

How we respond to adversity defines us and either causes us to expand who we are or to contract behind a shield of self-pity. The Lord's end game for us during such times is not just to endure, but to eventually rise up to our full height as real men. This may take years or a lifetime, but that is his solid goal.

God seemingly did not lift a finger to help Jesus during his time of severe hunger and brutal temptation while in the desert. And yet Jesus kept his eyes fixed on things above. He did not falter and, as a consequence, started his ministry with real power in the full knowledge of who he was as God's Son.[34]

I hate the saying, 'It is what it is.' It's so defeatist, so lacking in faith that the God of the impossible is in charge.

Let us, as sleeping giants, awake. Arise to be what we are meant to be – game-changers, world-altering awesome princes belonging to God Almighty, even in adversity.

If you fall to pieces in a crisis, there wasn't much
to you in the first place.
Proverbs 24:10, *The Message*

Chapter Twenty
A Growing Community

World Events

- The Chernobyl nuclear reactor explodes in the USSR
- *The Oprah Winfrey* Show debuts
- In New Zealand, Goods and Service Tax (GST) is introduced
- Our lovely son, Simon Carey, is born

Nora Ephron, the writer, said: 'A child is a grenade. When you have a baby, you set off an explosion in your marriage, and when the dust settles, your marriage is different from what is was.'[35]

Like us, I wonder how many couples thought their first baby would instantly conform to life's pattern as a tag-on to the carefree days of being married without children. Then reality explodes.

After my accident, our next move towards community living was to buy the three-bedroom villa together – a 'do-er-upper' in a good street. The house was not particularly big with five occupants but soon got smaller once we ripped one side of it apart. Many of the rooms were out of action for months as the layout altered, then morphed and then changed again. If a wall got in the way - out it came; if one didn't exist - we put one up.

To be fair, Nicholas did the lion's share of the endless bash and crash as I was still delicate after my back troubles. The man was a marvel; nothing seemed impossible with Nicholas by my side. For him every challenge was just a tea break.

Backing up the story, once I recovered from my stint in hospital, Sara and I had a bit of fun trying to conceive. After eight months all that was delivered was worry. The joke about 'Low Count Carey' and 'Barren von Sam' (her nickname) no longer seemed amusing with my bike accident and Sara's teenage anorexia weighing heavily on our minds.

That Christmas all five of us – including Nicholas and Michelle's daughter, Zoe – holidayed in a wonderful part of New Zealand called Ruby Bay near Nelson in the South Island. Sara felt queasy after the ferry trip but blamed the ham on the bone we had been devouring. Green ham or not, we were still cash-strapped so ate slices of it with almost every meal.

On New Year's Eve, Nicholas and I set off on a boys' trip to do some fly fishing. Actually, Nicholas fished while I trotted behind, but I didn't mind. Sara and I had started learning to fish for trout, so it was good to be in the presence of the master while enjoying spectacular rivers. Just when we agreed it was time to head back to celebrate the New Year with the girls, Nicholas latched onto a whopper. After a short but intense fight, the big fish got away but we were hooked, chasing the monster downriver through the twilight and well into the night.

Oblivious to time during the great pursuit, we eventually got back to our holiday home well after midnight. The clock in the car told us of our sin but we naively thought the three girls would be peacefully asleep and only a little disappointed. Boom – wrong again. The two older ones were up and no longer resembled serene loving wives – they had somehow grown in stature and ferocity (which is no mean feat as Michelle is only four foot ten and three-quarter inches).

Needless to say, we were collectively and individually scolded like two naughty schoolboys who were out late, who knows where, without telling anyone or showing any consideration for worried loved ones. All this was true.

Sara's well-directed tirade ended with a final blow when she said, 'What if I was pregnant and you had died?' It was then that we had an 'aha' moment; maybe, just maybe, the nausea that had persisted was more than just a lamb-ham moment.

Her wrath gradually turned to joy (too slowly if you ask an embarrassed me). Sure enough, once back in Wellington, the tests confirmed that Sara was newly pregnant with our very own bun in the oven.

Overcome with relief, we splashed out on a bottle of bubbly and headed up the coast to where Sara's parents were building a holiday home. Pop the builder also knew no bounds to his building projects, but having built a garage and several extensions this was his first venture constructing a complete house.

By coincidence he was putting the final touches to the roof when we arrived. Leaping from the ladder (and to conclusions) he thought the bubbly was part of the traditional 'roof shout'. We will never forget the surprised look on their faces when Sara said, 'Well, no, it's to celebrate you becoming grandparents.'

At one extreme, pregnancy is said to be like a third sex – with so many physical changes happening and hormones floating around the bearer is neither completely female or male. This was not so for Sara. For me things were hard work, coping with a new job and renovating a house while adjusting to living in a community, but for her being pregnant seemed easy.

Like most new parents-to-be, we relished each stage of development. The thought of this unknown person about to steal our hearts and change our lives forever was overwhelming at times. The concept of new life growing inside its loving host was both enthralling and unnerving.

God made it so that we need reciprocal relationships on all sorts of levels to flourish and to be healthy. His own relationship with us is the same. Although he doesn't need us, we breathe and exist because he chooses to allow it. But the wonderful thing is that he also chooses that we should be his much-loved children; he wants us to find freedom from everything that would hold us back from growing into who we are meant to be.

Sara's constant glow as the ideal expectant mum dimmed somewhat in the last month. We were the second parents of our antenatal group due to give birth, but each night I would find her in tears because another friend had popped out a beautiful baby while we were left waiting. Like all desperate parents-to-be, we tried everything to bring on the birth.

Funnily enough, the only thing that worked was the one and only time Sara mowed the lawns in our entire married life. There she was, hugely pregnant, waddling behind a lawnmower and muttering to herself, 'This had better work or else.'

It did and that evening was to be the night of my life. It started slowly and calmly as Sara woke saying the time had come. Not wanting to wake Michelle, Nicholas and Zoe, we moved into the lounge for what was supposed to be the long haul of labour. Then to my surprise her mood quickly shifted for the worse – as did the contractions. The suddenness of the change triggered a flashback to those gruelling antenatal videos, especially the one when the woman gets angry at her partner as she goes through transition, signalling that the birth is imminent.

I insisted we leave for the hospital and bundled my protesting wife into our communal van, driving as fast as I dared. At the maternity ward, as I valiantly leapt out of the van to get help, I leaned on the horn. The prolonged burst of sound brought the midwives running.

I am sure the hospital staff thought I was a panicking first-time father. Instead of rushing, their initial action was to calmly send Sara to the lavatory. This mistake nearly ended up with our baby being born in the toilet bowl as Sara was so ready to birth. When they finally got around to checking her they were amazed to find she was very dilated (whatever that means). After a rush to the birthing suite a bouncing baby boy was born twenty minutes later, following a couple of superhuman pushes. The total labour was a mere two and a half hours long.

I can't describe the feeling of witnessing my child being born. It's a whirl of elation that it's over, wonder at seeing a miracle, worry over squashed features and concern for your poor wife. It's a mess and yet it is the most beautiful thing you will ever see.

When I could finally pry myself away, I drove through the streets of Petone with the window down shouting, '*Yahoo*, I'm a dad', to anyone awake and everyone asleep.

The sun was just coming up and the sunrise was magnificent beyond belief. I stopped at a petrol station to buy some cigars and discovered that the attendant was a member of our antenatal group. Of course, he was already a dad which meant he was probably responsible for one of my wife's tearful episodes. Nevertheless, he made up for it by giving me the cigars free of charge which topped off the most marvellous of nights.

When I got home, I slid happily back into bed, and put some worship music on my Walkman. I was so wound up I couldn't sleep, but I didn't care. The music had never sounded so good and my many thoughts were buzzing like bees to a hive dripping with happiness.

My world had exploded and expanded at the same time. I was a dad. Life would never be the same. The grenade had gone off and I was glad. All I could think of was: 'Welcome to the world, Simon, my beautiful son.'

Message to men (MTM)

There is a cosmic battle happening that has been raging for eons. And it's about the hearts of fathers.

It all started when God created people in his image and called them his children. But they rebelled and walked away, forfeiting a relationship with him. Ever since then the Lord has ached over his children. The very essence of the gospel is about the Father's heart towards his estranged kids.

It should come as no surprise then that one of the primary tactics of the enemy, Satan, is to undermine the relationships that fathers have with their children. Once the word 'father' became synonymous with remote, uncaring, strict, unseen, then when we hear about God being our Father we automatically ascribe the same attributes to him.

I know because I did. And the idea of being a father myself scared me witless.

When I look at the proverb below I can't help think, 'What if I wasn't around to train my children – to be a positive role model for them?' The answer is clearly articulated in endless research which shows that children without a father at home are at a higher risk of getting involved in all kinds of undesirable things like substance abuse, violence, dropping out of school, and pre-material pregnancies. However, what is worse is the high rate of mental health issues.

The real story here is one of prodigal fathers running from the responsibilities of parenting and commitment. Men, we have a vital role to play as fathers in a great battle for the well-being of our children and our nation.

Start children off on the way they should go, and even when they are old they will not turn from it.
Proverbs 22:6

Chapter Twenty-One
Little Nation

World Events

- 'The Simpsons' make their debut on *The Tracy Ullman Show*
- Māori becomes New Zealand's second official language
- Sara and Simon head to England leaving me very lonely

For nearly seven years we had been a little nation of two. But then our borders were crossed by an invader whom we welcomed with open arms. Somehow this tiny disrupter seemed to have always belonged. Simon was part of us now and very quickly we couldn't imagine life without him.

As with all foreigners, communication is difficult at first, but we learned in a hurry as his protesting cries were somehow connected to our heart strings. We were bewildered and bleary-eyed new parents who found life tiring, but to our amazement it was also very rewarding.

That year was crammed full of firsts; all of them little and insignificant to the untrained eye but to us, and to anyone who would listen to these besotted parents, each first was as remarkable as if it had never happened before.

Simon stole my heart from the moment he was born, and the joy of knowing him seemed without bounds. The first time he smiled I was ecstatic with joy. In return, I grinned so hard and long that my face ached like it had on my wedding day.

Yes, a grenade had gone off, but when the dust settled we found we loved being parents. We were deeply touched by how vulnerable this baby was and how dependent he was on us for every aspect of his well-being.

Life became very busy – way beyond what we had foolishly calculated. All the while renovations were going on and I was struggling with being the manager at Fantail Computing with seven staff who needed to be paid each fortnight. Little Jeremy – Nicholas and Michelle's son – was born six weeks after Simon which saw our community grow from five to seven people, shoehorned into a three-bedroom semi-functioning building site. Our place was hardly a peaceful nursery for three little ones under three.

One afternoon, Sara came home from shopping and placed Simon on the coffee table in his car seat. She hoped he would continue to sleep so scurried out the door to do 1,000 things in 100 seconds during those rare baby downtimes. Simon obliged by promptly falling off the table and onto some timber, which was waiting to become part of the new-look home.

The heart-wrenching scream saw Sara racing back to a blooded baby with a cut above his right eye. My wife is a calm, level-headed person but on that day, I got a call from a blubbering wreck of a mother who could hardly speak in coherent sentences.

An urgent ride to the doctor confirmed he was unharmed except for a nice shiner for all and sundry to tut about. More tears ensued when I got home – not from the hurt party who seemed happy and full of smiles to see his dad, but from his emotionally battered mother. That day we learned that to even slightly injure one so vulnerable and so fully under your care is a truly disturbing experience.

When Simon was just six weeks old and still a newborn, we decided to take him on a road trip to meet his other set of grandparents. Still stuck in the old ways of thinking when we were a nation of two, we combined the trip with taking a yacht up the centre of the island to Nicholas's parents' and then going across to Napier where my parents lived. What were we thinking?

The trip was big enough by New Zealand standards, but made harder by towing a large boat behind a gutless van across the Desert Road. What made it almost impossible was expecting a newborn to also toe the line.

Our usually happy baby boy was utterly miserable. Having barely survived the journey up to see my folks, the trip home saw him screaming the last two hours despite our best efforts to comfort him. And every parent knows what comes next – he fell asleep just as we pulled into the driveway. We were shattered with ground-down nerves, travelling fatigue and lack of quality sleep, but he was peacefully snoozing as if nothing much had happened. Kids are more robust than we give them credit for.

The biggest event of the year came about when my in-laws suggested that Lesley and Sara take Simon to the UK to show him off to their relatives. It was an opportunity not to be missed as several of Sara's cousins also had babies and toddlers and were conveniently living within a few miles of each other. The gathering of the tiny clan-nites became part of family legend.

Things were settled without discussion; Sara and Simon were to go to England, paid for by her generous parents, and I was to stay at home.

My gorgeous boy was eleven months when he left and did not return until he was a walking one-year-old. Communication was slim; no one had bothered to invent email or Facebook and international toll calls were still difficult and expensive.

I found myself once more haunted by having to wait for letters from my beloved. Despite living in a community, I felt a constant ache and harrowing loneliness. Two of the three pieces that had come to define the essence of me were missing.

So it was that I missed my firstborn's first birthday. If that wasn't cruel enough, I was not there when he took his first steps in jolly ol' England. I cried the night I heard that piece of news.

As I write this, I am touched by the irony of it all. Thirty years later that same lad is overseas, this time in Norway with his wife and one of my much-loved grandsons. The thing is, Jakob turned one while there and with history repeating itself, I missed this important event. Like son, like grandson.

On his actual birthday, I wrote Simon a letter which then became a tradition for each of our children during the early years of their lives. Highlights went like this:

Today you are one year old, my son. On this day I celebrate not only your first year of life but a year of joy and blessing that you have brought to me. In the spectrum of life, we hardly know each other but I have loved you since the night you were born. Your life is a precious gift to me, given by the

FATHER, the author of life. You are given to me for a time to love, to disciple, to enjoy, to make deep friends with. I want you to know now, at the beginning of your life, that your mum and I have only two things we want for you.

We want you to be happy and to be our friend. Neither of these two things can be [fully] achieved if you do not know our Father of Joy, our true friend. Simon, it has been prophesied that one day you will be like Simon Peter the Rock … a teacher of men with the gift of intelligence and understanding.

But for now you are just one, my little baby…

… Although you were brand new, you knew us and we knew you. Everything about your birth was special and that is no accident.

Since then you have always been strong and full of joy, as one day you will be a mighty man of God, strong in knowledge and revelation. But I say to you now while you are young, it will not be easy. Simon Michael – like Simon Peter, you will have to be disciplined and your strong will tamed in the ways of the kingdom.

That task falls to me, your father. For a time, you are completely under my earthly and spiritual authority. The Lord has said that I will be made strong to bring you up in strength too. There will be times in your life where you think my making you happy and making you my friend is the opposite of what I really intend. We will hurt each other but one day you will uncover real happiness and immeasurable friendship with me. But [we will] pay a price for it and there will be hard times in our friendship.

However, today you are just one. And in your first year of life you have given me one of the best years I have had in the twenty-nine I have lived so far. I love you, Simon, and I count it a great privilege to be your father. Already you are much more than I could ever have hoped for. You have made my life blessed.

Well, Simon, although you are many miles away, in England, on your first birthday nothing can weaken our friendship on this day. I can only look forward to celebrating even more birthdays with you, each year becoming more blessed because of you. Your friend and dad.

Message to men (MTM)

When I look around the church I sometimes think, how can I have more capacity to open my life up to others? I'm maxed out.

That's how I felt before Simon was born. By then I had been in love with Sara for around nine years. My heart was bursting with love for her alone. How then could I make room for some stranger?

Love is one of those mysteriously limitless things. We are not given finite portions that somehow run out when we use it up.

We men were born for love. How do I know that? Well, we were created in God's image and he is love.[36]

To love others as we love the Lord is what gives us meaning and purpose as he designed.

So, make the effort and open your hearts and lives to others. It's not a flowery wishy-washy sentiment. A man who does not love is not a real man.

> *Unfriendly people care only about themselves ...*
> Proverbs 18:1, NLT

Chapter Twenty-Two
Defining Choices

World Events

- Wall Street crashes leading to billions being wiped of the value of shares worldwide
- *The Princess Bride* hits theatres and becomes an instant classic
- The NZ All Blacks win the inaugural Rugby World Cup
- I decide that being a family for God is more important that starting my own business

I am told that every time you blink the brain keeps things illuminated so the world doesn't go dark. With a new baby to entertain a willing audience of two, my small world was full of life, laughter and wonder. But I blinked a few times that year which could have ended in darkness.

A defining event happened early on when I changed jobs. Sounds ordinary enough, but put in context I was faced with a life-changing choice.

As a start-up company, Fantail Computing was more than exciting. Personal Computers were the new revolution of the mid-1980s. Apple Macs had burst onto the scene, but without the broad software base of Microsoft. Our little company could barely keep up with the demand to sell hardware, write software and train users. Fantail Computing had a burgeoning number of customers, some of whom were hard men like loan sharks and butchers.

At times, we became overcommitted and some of my staff foolishly made promises they couldn't keep. One of my more disturbing memories was that of a loan shark barging into my office with the obligatory henchmen who immediately stood on either side of me, dwarfing my puny six foot two stature.

Despite these kinds of hiccups, we were good at what we did and were considering marketing our software in Australia. The interest was high and the outlay small once we wrote the code.

I was young and inexperienced, but I knew instinctively that cashflow was king so I managed it well. The problem was that we were part of a small group of two companies owned by two of the biggest cowboys outside Texas.

How Howard and Keith ever got together is a mystery. Howard was slick, and everything about him screamed 'salesman'. Ethics were optional, sales were everything and he dressed and acted the part to perfection. He was a 'blow the expense, give the cat another goldfish' kind of guy and I suspect this is what got the company into trouble as they leased cars, took on office space, hired loads of staff and generally lived as if work didn't come before success.

Several times I went cold calling with Howard as part of my training. In the early days this was done using our little Mini, which frequently wouldn't start. I have vivid memories of my highly pregnant wife having to push the car so I could crash start it to avoid being late for appointments.

Once there, I would weigh up whether what we were selling was truly suitable for the client. Being 'honest Lon', I regarded genuineness and relationship as the cornerstone of sales and still do. I sometimes walked away from a sale, at which point Howard would be furious at me. If it wasn't for the fact that I was being groomed to take over running Fantail Computing, I think he would have fired me. However, just before I abandoned working in sales and moved full-time to management, I scored the highest number of sales among the team for the month. Who says honesty doesn't pay?

Keith, on the other hand, was a hippie, a weirdy-beardy of old but also a bit of a genius with computers. But like most uber-bright people, he had a magpie mindset where he seldom finished things due to the distractions of something new and shiny taking his attention.

It seemed impossible to count Keith's children, as they were numerous and ran wild. Keith and his wife worked in both businesses and would often just leave the kids in the car for hours on end as a way of containing them. Sympathetic staff would check on them every now and then, but the smell inside the car was unbearable as was the cacophony that rose from the overcrowded vehicle.

Inevitably, the mother company got into strife and before long the directors were robbing my cash to pay their staff. When I refused to sign the cheques, they threatened to remove me as a signatory. I knew from the little business acumen I had that the slope was almost vertical at this stage, and that both companies would fold within a month.

Fantail Computing had seven staff who needed to gather food for another twenty hungry mouths. It just wasn't sustainable, so I resigned. To my surprise the directors countered with an offer of making me managing director across both companies. Flattered but suspicious, I insisted on seeing the books. Reluctantly they agreed and within minutes I knew their fate was carved in stone.

I was now faced with one of the biggest decisions in my life. Should I take the software programmers with me and form my own company? Judging by the success of other IT companies that started during this decade I probably would have been a multimillionaire by now. But at what cost?

Start-up companies are not for the timid, or for those who easily give up. I was neither of these, but deep down I also knew they demanded your entire attention and all your energy. Most of all what they needed was momentum and that didn't happen unless the company had the best of you, whenever it was necessary.

The same can be said of being a new parent. It's a start-up venture not for the diffident or the quitters. To be successful it requires the best of you, any time of day or night.

Already, while sole charge manager of Fantail Computing, I was in the habit of going to work early. Since it was only a short distance from home, I would spend my lunchtimes alongside my family pacing up and down, worrying out loud, and eating a lunch I couldn't remember.

After a token kiss to my wife and son I would race back to work until late. Even then I would bring home one of the sparkly new Apple Macs to carry on working in the evening – most evenings.

When I told Sara I was thinking of starting my own company using the existing talent from Fantail Computing and creaming off the best of the customers, she said something that would change my thinking forever. My wonderful wife said, 'You promised me all those years ago when we had no children that when the time came you would be there as a father.'

At this point in time I had my own Big Bang moment and became a new creation. I was pioneering a new path already laden with success with the promise of fortune. At that moment I knew I was also on a route to becoming a habitually absent and preoccupied parent.

Fatherhood was not a natural fit for me as I had always been fearful of being a dad. My own background did not leave me with positive role models – growing up, my world was disjointed and messy. By the time my mother died she had had six boys to four fathers and had been married four times. My biological father had also been married three times. I was a victim of this situation and was profoundly afraid of history repeating itself. It took years of being a Christian and slowly gaining a firm grasp of who I was as a child of God to realise that in Jesus the chain was broken. In him I became a victor.

I had a choice – be there for Simon or be there for my business. I chose Simon and am so thankful that I did. Today our relationship and the relationship I have with all my children is very special. Through years of investment into them, they have grown from being my beloved children to becoming my friends. They are part of the sacred inner circle of those I trust and I value their advice and support beyond most others.

The chain has been broken and in time I became the parent I wished my father had been. I got involved and it was great fun.

And now I have the incredible privilege of experiencing the same with my grandchildren. I chose to be there as an integral part of my children's life and it is the best investment I have ever made. The returns are locked away in our memories as treasures for eternity.

Message to men (MTM)

What is real power?

It was said of John the Baptist that he would 'go on before the Lord, in the spirit and power of Elijah' (Luke 1:17) and yet there is no record of him ever performing miracles. Did the Bible get it wrong? Was the angel who delivered this message only talking figuratively?

What John did do was to turn people's hearts towards God, by the thousands. Now, that's power in its ultimate form.

When Jesus said, 'What is impossible with man is possible with God' (Luke 18:27), he was not referring to acts of speculator miracles. No, he was referring to a change in heart for the rich young ruler. This is what seemed impossible.

For me, real power was having the chain broken that bound me to generations of broken marriages and poor fathering.

Real power is about being transformed from the inside out, becoming a brand-new being in Christ and choosing to stay that way for the rest of your life.

Above all else, guard your heart, for everything
you do flows from it.
Proverbs 4:23

Chapter Twenty-Three
Blackest Darkness

World Events
- Photoshop is made available to the public
- After illegally jumping from the Eiffel Tower, A.J. Hackett begins the world's first commercial bungy jump near Queenstown, NZ
- We are attending a cult

I blinked and had almost given my life over to the deity of work. Thanks to the wisdom of my wife, I avoided that walk of darkness which would see me become but a shadow in my own house.

That was bad enough, like drifting onto rocks while following a meretricious beacon, but worse was to come, the blackest darkness. Our little community unwittingly blundered into becoming members of what in my opinion was a cult.

Our dreams of a large communal house on a big piece of land were shattered thanks to my back accident. Therefore, we found ourselves in a holding pattern, renovating the house to raise capital and having babies while we waited. Our idealistic plan was to free resources so the four adults could work with others in want. In the right circumstances you do not always need two people to look after the children or two full incomes when your needs are kept low and everything is shared. Thus, we could allow members of our community to be deeply involved in the lives of others, unshackled from the demands of young children and challenging careers.

In a leap of trust in each other and faith in God we pooled all our resources, including money. Nicholas had started a business with Michelle's uncle which was based in our garage, but we were all shareholders. I was the only one providing a steady income, working for the Fire Service.

None of us were satisfied with the lack of passion in our faith. All eagerly desired to be part of some kind of radical Christianity that made a difference and was authentic.

So it was that we were ripe for the picking when we heard about this newly formed church. The first meeting we attended was amazing. The people were friendly, we had never heard such powerful preaching and they had a lunch after the service at which they enfolded us by making room and sharing their food.

Things were different to say the least. No chairs were put out in the school hall. Everyone just stood, or danced and sang until the sermon when we sat. The ladies wore headscarves, but didn't seem unhappy. There were prophecies, scripture readings, pictures – all the things that are normal today in charismatic churches, but three decades ago it was awesome to experience after years of mainstream monotony.

All four adults came home that day abuzz with excitement. Had we finally found a church on fire, white-hot for God? In retrospect, we were blinded by our desperation for something more, something closer to the extraordinary norms found on almost every page of the New Testament.

During the next few weeks, I questioned the seemingly approachable elders over why the headscarves and why the formal attire worn by a lot of the congregation. I was told it fitted well with scripture[37] that women needed to show visible submission to their husbands. The wearing of your Sunday best was because we were in the house of God. The argument continued that we wouldn't come before a king in jeans. Being an ex-hippie, I couldn't buy that and I countered that surely we are before God the King no matter where we are, and that Sundays are about coming together as the family of God. I remembered stories told by Pop that made me shudder of how he had had to come before his father at dinnertimes wearing a jacket and tie, and how distant he felt from him.

All that submission stuff also grated on me; in Malachi 2:14 and 1 Peter 3:7 it clearly states that Sara is my life partner. I know you can't have a democracy of two, but true partnership is serving each other in love and respect. This church emphasised wives needing to submit to husbands but overlooked Ephesians 5:21 about submitting 'to one another', which comes first.

It wasn't long before I had a visit from the pastor who was seemingly weighing up each marriage on the submission front. Those wives found wanting were labelled 'Jezebels' and the husbands given clear instruction on how to assert their authority. I objected long and loud to anyone calling Sara a Jezebel.

Yes, she is spirited and sometimes feisty, but ours was a marriage built out of hard work – we valued Team Carey above all else. Just like the quote from the Bible in Proverbs 27:17 about iron sharpening iron, we had filed off many of our rough edges to the point where we valued each other's opinions beyond token submission.

Surprisingly, my questioning this and other matters earned me a special place among the elite. The pastor offered to spend one-on-one time with me on a weekly basis, going over the preaching and looking carefully at what the Bible had to say. Each Thursday I came home early from work and would cruise round to his home where we discussed matters at great length.

He told me I was being groomed for leadership and that I was to feel free to question everything he said. So I did. But it was not long before I saw the monster hiding behind those slick words that came so easily to him.

I must admit this kind of talk tickled my ears and puffed me up somewhat. To my shame when I look back on my diaries of the day, they talk about taking charge of my household before I can lead in the church, and establishing my authority over Sara. There are cruel words about Sara submitting and me being loving (as if that justifies dominating another).

This all sounds good if you say it fast enough, but underneath it all was something sinister. On the positive side, I think by echoing the pastor's words on paper I began to see that something was very wrong.

The other elders were lovely men of God, but cowed down by the pastor. Very early on, one of them, a forthright man who knew his God, mysteriously left the church. The other elder had a wonderful gentle and caring spirit.

When baby Simon was just a few months old we dedicated him at church and this elder bought the most amazing prophecy when he said, 'Simon, we won't be disappointed if you are anything like Simon Peter, the rock. You will rise up a teacher, have an enquiring mind and curiosity. You won't just teach learned knowledge but also revelation. I give you a blessing of intelligence and understanding.'

My wee boy was just ten weeks old then and his personality unknown. Yet to know him thirty years later you would be stunned by how true those words of prophecy were.

With one elder gone, the pastor appointed another, a henchman to be his enforcer. After that things deteriorated. The dynamic duo of the henchman and the pastor visited every couple to discuss broader, more intrusive topics, such as how much money couples were giving to the church, whether the elders thought it wise to have babies, or buy houses, or change jobs. The level of control increased significantly along with my unease.

The step too far came when the pastor preached about special revelation God had given him. He bare-facedly stated that compared to everyone else he was 80 per cent pure light and that even the most mature person in the church, other than him, was only 20 per cent. God had told him that he alone would bring direct revelation from God and that we must listen to it. You can imagine my session with him that week. There are so many scriptures that refute this kind of false teaching that it's laughable. Needless to say, the pastor was very upset by my challenge.

His message was strongly reinforced by another bizarre Sunday brainwashing when he told everyone that God had said he would preach beyond what was in the Bible, heavily implying that the Bible would become secondary to his teachings. This time it was me who was angry. I love the Bible and always have done since first becoming a Christian. I devour it daily. My current version is crammed full of notes. Everything in me screamed that this new teaching was wrong, and I had many scriptures to back up the dangers of going beyond what is written in the Word of God.

Very soon after that infamous session, I received a letter saying that I was a waste of the pastor's time, God had given me the chance to take on board what he was revealing but I had not embraced it. Unless I did, the Spirit of God would soon pass me by.

Like Sara, I can be feisty too, and I responded with a letter outlining all my concerns about the pastor and the church. Eyewitnesses loyal to me reported that he laughed when handed it, and then made a spectacle of ripping it up unread and throwing it in the bin.

That was it, I was doomed. From that moment on I was labelled an outcast and the church instructed not to talk to me. Secretly Michelle and Nicholas were coached to watch everything we did and to report back to the elders.

When you are in a negative frame of mind, you tend to see everything through those distorted lenses. Even positive things somehow get overlooked or misconstrued. And so it was within our community; there were secrets, and clandestine discussions about us and suspicion over everything we said or did.

Sara and I persisted in the church. I don't know why; maybe it was for the sake of our friendship with Michelle and Nicholas. But the community itself imploded and after a devastating argument between Sara and Nicholas, it ended. Sara took me for a long stroll along the beach and said she couldn't do life like this anymore, she felt she was constantly walking on eggshells throughout the day.

After three years, it was over. The shattered pieces of our dreams were blown away by the winds of suspicion and dissension. The amazing thing was that the break-up, which was not unlike a divorce, was amicable to the point of hilarious. We argued over who got what, not for ourselves but to the benefit of the others.

The hardest part for me was leaving Zoe and baby Jeremy. They were like close family members to me. I had a special relationship with Jeremy who was a ratbag for everyone else but not for me. That Sunday I hugged him so hard that he whimpered with discomfort. I cried a lot regarding the loss of Jeremy as I knew that Michelle and Nicholas would have to distance themselves from us, and indeed had done so already.

We moved in with Sara's generous parents in Wellington's Island Bay, and the darkness descended on me. During that time, I turned thirty and Sara made me a lion cake symbolic of a precious postcard she had sent me soon after I had first asked her out. Even that didn't console me. Simon was two and to my gloomy amusement he was a great source of comfort. Somehow, he knew his daddy was deeply sad and his kind heart saw him take every opportunity to try to cheer me up.

Of course, that's not the end of the story about church. Soon after, the pastor, emboldened by his recent prophecies about himself, told the congregation that God had revealed to him that three miracles would occur. He stated that if they did not come to pass the church was to dismiss him as pastor and to regard him as a fake. One of those miracles involved a little diabetic girl. The parents took him at his word and removed her from insulin treatment. Tragically she died, despite pleading with her parents to give her the drugs. They were prosecuted. The pastor was interviewed by the police but no fault was found in him.

You may wonder how he justified it to the congregation. The pastor added to the mother's grief by reportedly labelling her a witch and putting the entire blame on her. This was too much for many in the church and a slow exodus started, including Michelle and Nicholas. Soon after, there was a marvellous reconciliation between the four of us where we hugged and forgave each other through real tears of love and sorrow.

Years later we would occasionally meet with ex-members of the church, including the original elders. Each one had a story to tell about escaping the church as if escaping through fire. Without exception, they all started their tale by saying, 'You realise, of course, that it was a cult.'

God's Spirit hadn't passed me by, Jesus promised never to leave or forsake me.[38] But I had lost the light in my life and was living under the shadow of dark despair. I was deeply saddened by all that had happened. Daily life seemed heavy and meaningless and dark. This almost cost me everything, had it not been for God orchestrating an unusual series of events.

Message to men (MTM)

So, men, what are the warning signs regarding supposed cults? It can be subtle to begin with as things don't always start off this way.

First and foremost, the cult centres around the leader. Their leadership is authoritarian and they demand obedience. Typically, the leader is not accountable to anyone else outside of the cult. Questioning is discouraged and seen as rebellious; it may even be punished.

There is often 'heavy shepherding', interfering with people's life decisions and personal choices.

Over time the cult develops a strong sense of elitism. Members genuinely believe they are the only ones who are right and that they hold a special place in God's eyes. They are exclusive in that they are seldom open to having strangers attend.

Probably worst of all is that the leaders will begin to go beyond what is written in the Bible or focus on a specific subset of biblical teaching.

Lastly, there exists a strong fear of leaving the fellowship. Members often believe something dreadful will happen to them or that they will be exposed to demonic attack.

Every word of God is flawless; he is a shield to those who take refuge in him. Do not add to his words, or he will rebuke you and prove you a liar.
Proverbs 30:5-6

Chapter Twenty-Four
The Nat-Man

World Events

- The World Wide Web comes into being
- Nintendo Game Boy is born
- The ever-young Barbie doll turns thirty
- Our second son, Nat, is welcomed to the world

Last week my biological father died. I didn't go to his funeral; he wouldn't have wanted me to.

I wish I could say that I am really sad about this, but when reality bites the wounds were found to be superficial. I am completely unemotional about his death; neutral, in fact. I am not sure if this is my way of coping, or some sinister deep-seated way of taking revenge on a man who should have been part of my life, loving me unconditionally and being my biggest fan. That's what real dads do.

I said earlier that growing up in my family was messy and disjointed. Not so now. Contrast my numb reaction to my biological father's death with what happened within my own family. I was pastored by my middle son.

The Nat-Man, as we like to call him, is now twenty-nine years old and has a wonderful cheery wife, two amazingly cute sons and a baby daughter. He works part-time for the church and, when I wrote this, as a geologist. On both counts his life is full of 'rocks' which he is passionate about.

Nat contacted me immediately on hearing the news about my father and then took me for a walk and a talk to a coffee shop. He could sense I wasn't too bereaved so he let me pay for his hot chocolate and my flat white.

We chatted away with the ease of lifelong friends who have a common foundation on which they have built their lives. When needed Nat slipped in words of wisdom and encouragement, but mostly he just actively listened. In contrast to my relationship with my father, I came away feeling truly loved and believing that my own son was my biggest fan.

The Nat-Man has always been special, but for a while there was a distinct possibility that he would not make it into this world. Back in 1989, when Sara was well into her pregnancy with him, she began to bleed. Immediately she was confined to bed, which is no easy thing when you have an active toddler to care for as well.

Although we had remained in the so-called cult, we had by then moved into a house in Lower Hutt. After months of searching, this place had popped up by 'accident'. Every time Sara found a suitable house to buy, Mr Negative would find something wrong – a dark cloud was still hanging over me which I couldn't shake. My poor wife would spend hours dragging a toddler around likely houses only to have me dismiss them with a callous wave of my hand and without proper dialogue.

In despair, she went to have coffee with a friend from our university days. Sue mentioned that the house next door was for sale and amazingly I loved it, as did Sara. After taking on a mortgage at 16½ per cent interest, we moved in.

This so-called 'accident' was the start of a series of events which saved my soul, but that's the subject of the next chapter. For now, we are focusing on the Nat-Man.

With Sara confined to rest, I was compelled to bring her tea and toast every morning. My canny wife rather liked this routine. Twenty-nine years later I am still making her a cuppa each morning to get her fuelled for the day.

In more recent times, we drink our tea together in bed while we have our own daily Bible readings. We may then share something inspirational that has grabbed us – a thought for the day – and then pray together for a few minutes. Our prayers are invariably about our family. We decided some time ago to be prayer warriors on their behalf, and of course every family has daily, if not hourly, dramas that we need to bring before God.

On Saturdays, if we haven't had little grandsons to sleep over, we will make toast and a large pot of real coffee and then read the paper from cover to cover while still in bed. It seems that one small tradition leads to others.

Sara did recover from the bleeding, but decided that she needed to stay healthy for this baby. Despite it being autumn, she would get up before me (I thought she was bewitched as this was unheard of) and go to our local school where she would swim lengths of the pool. The water was freezing and I remember chuckling aloud many times when she came back looking like she wasn't even pregnant. Poor baby Nat would bury himself deep inside her to stay warm.

When the final month of pregnancy came around, my determined wife was extremely fit. However, those last four weeks proved to be as tortuous as her pregnancy with Simon. This time she began having frequent Braxton Hicks contractions. These not-so-jolly contractions are a bit like a dress rehearsal and are hard to distinguish from real labour. Consequently, I often thought the baby was on its way when he wasn't, which cost me dearly in credibility.

At first, this had both of us and Lesley on high alert; Sara was keen that her mother be present this time. Judging by my antics the first time (like waking the entire hospital by falling on the horn of the van), I think she was probably wise. But as the weeks went by, we just got used to the Braxton Hicks and relaxed a bit too much. Sara's mum was staying with us, but the waiting and watching was taking its toll, so Sara sent Lesley home, some forty-five minutes' drive away.

On a frigid night in early May, Sara woke me to say her waters had broken. I wanted to be more alert and calm this time so I said I would have a shower. 'Fine,' she said. 'It will be hours anyway.'

There I was, absentmindedly soaping myself down, while unbeknown to me Sara was in heavy labour. When I got out of the shower, I was shocked to find her about to give birth. I rang Sue, who lived next door, Lesley, and then an ambulance. Sue arrived within seconds and we placed Sara on the carpet in the lounge in front of the gas heater. Within minutes, I caught the baby as Sara did one final push.

Here I was, this slippery creature in my hands with both ladies squealing at me, 'Well, is it a boy or a girl?' Still in shock

I mumbled, 'I don't know –the cord is in the way.' More retorts were volleyed at me, 'Well, move it and see, dopey.'

Luckily for us the doctor had briefed us on what to do if we had an accidental home birth; he had been seriously impressed with our first child's two-and-a-half-hour delivery. Dutifully, we wrapped Nat in a towel and laid him on Sara's stomach while we waited for the ambulance. Every time he cried we comforted him, and every time he was quiet we gently shook him until he cried.

The hospital was actually visible from our place, but it still took twenty minutes for the ambulance to arrive. I cheerily greeted them at the gate telling them the baby had been born, at which they sprinted inside. After a bit of fussing, they tied the cord and asked me if I wanted to have the honour of cutting it. I did, although I disliked separating something that had once been the source of life between my beloved wife and our cherished child.

Sara's meteoric claim to fame was that the entire labour, from waters breaking to the arrival of the Nat-Man, took a mere twelve minutes. My lame claim to fame was that most of this time I had spent in the shower.

Lesley arrived just as we were piling into the ambulance. Quickly asking her to look after Simon and adding, 'It's a boy,' we waved her goodbye and we sped off on our one-minute drive to the hospital. Several hours later, when I could finally tear myself away from my truly amazing wife and adorable second son, I walked home full of a joy that I had not known for some time.

As I came in the door Lesley flung herself into my arms, totally distressed and weepy. It is true to say that you see things differently from where you are standing. In her case, she had got an urgent call to come quickly; having arrived she saw her daughter and new grandson being bundled into an ambulance without a word of explanation. Putting two and two together she came up with five and concluded that things had gone horribly wrong.

In fact, the opposite was true. Our miracle baby boy, whom we had nearly lost, had come into the world with gusto and strength. His lightning-fast twelve-minute birth was to become typical of the speed and efficiency by which he leads his life – always full-on, always exciting.

Here we are, all these years later, and the same boy is now pastoring his dad and, in true Nat-Man style, doing it superbly well.

Message to men (MTM)

I have been asked, 'What has this chapter got to do with marriage?' The answer is: 'Everything.' My life goal is to be a family for God. I desire to see my children 'standing on the shoulders of Giants',[39] building on all the good things that the previous generation of believers has accomplished and fought hard for.

The root to all this is my relationship with Sara. Marriage is many things, but some of those things revolve around being an enabler for others to flourish.

When you are truly loved and cherished and you fully grasp who you are, the strength of that self-awareness enables you to be all that you are meant to be. This is the crux of Christian living and it is reflected in family life under God.

This chapter is about my son caring for me, in a sense, fathering me. He stands tall, head and shoulders above many of the spiritual giants of my day. And I believe a lot of this has to do with all the good things that Sara and I have jointly put into his life.

Truly, the best thing I could ever do for my children is to love my wife.

Her children respect and bless her; her husband joins in with words of praise: 'Many women have done wonderful things, but you've outclassed them all!'
Proverbs 31:28-29, *The Message*

Chapter Twenty-Five
Run Away Jonah

World Events

- The first GPS satellite goes into orbit
- The Berlin wall comes down
- We leave the cult and try to move to Hong Kong

Nearly 300 years ago Heinrich Heine said, 'One should forgive one's enemies, but not before they are hanged.'[40]

Nat was born and we were still part of the alleged cult, clutching on by our fingertips. But when the pastor publicly congratulated Sara on the arrival of Nathaniel Carey and didn't mention me, it was the last of the 1,000 cuts that nearly killed my soul.

I was devastated by that simple act. Boldly I demanded the elders come to our house where I confronted them over asking Michelle and Nicholas to spy on us, seeking to split up the community and telling the congregation not to have anything to do with me. The pastor and the henchman revelled in telling me it was all true while the other elder said nothing.

I knew that as a Christian I should forgive them, but secretly I wanted to see them hanged first.

Later, the other elder came to me at church and shared one of his many encouraging words. He said, 'Have you ever played cricket? The Lord would have you know that no matter what you are going through, he is batting for you.' I broke down when I heard this and sobbed and sobbed.

Soon after, we left the suspected cult behind us, expecting that things would be better. But it felt to me that nothing was in our favour. The high interest mortgage was crippling us financially. Money was very tight and a constant source of tension. With Michelle and Nicholas off the scene I felt bereft of friendship. And somehow, I had a knack of attracting bizarre jobs that never made sense.

I had taken a role with the Fire Service National Headquarters as the information systems manager. The interview with the director was off the wall. He went on and on for one and half hours about the organisation and the systems, drawing endless diagrams on a whiteboard that were illegible while I sat there trying to not to embarrass myself by falling asleep. I hardly got to say a word. Very few of the ninety minutes concerned my relevant skills or experience, which I clearly did not have an abundance of anyway. The witty Heinrich Heine summed up my new boss when he said, 'There are more fools in the world than there are people.'[41]

Despite having two job offers on the table I decided to take the role with the Fire Service as the safe bet, since it was a quasi-government department. In 1987 I was the first of the Fire Service's permanent IT staff as the system had been set up by seven expensive consultants. My job was to singlehandedly replace them even though I knew nothing about the technology being used.

During my training, I accidentally took the entire system down after the consultant assured me this could never happen. He promptly left for lunch, leaving me to face the agitated hierarchy who must have been wondering what sort of goon they had just hired.

I didn't trust the consultants after that, and I had a nagging suspicion they were setting me up to look bad so that the Fire Service would rehire them. Their names were secretly added to those I must forgive once I had them hanged.

My dark mood continued and by the time Nat was born I had thrown myself into work like a man possessed. I was on twenty-four-hour call-out and had to come in during the weekends to do back-ups. This meant that Sara had no car for most of the weekend, making her life very hard, especially as she was trying to find us a new spiritual home as well.

Soon after Nat's arrival, I worked forty-two days without a single day off. Naturally, I was tired, negative and cranky. The good news is that when we are at the end of ourselves that's when God steps in.

Our new home was on a shared driveway servicing four houses. Within a few days of Nat's birth one of our neighbours visited, telling us about his faith and the church he went to. We were impressed by his gentle spirit and genuine nature, but I was too busy at work to be bothered.

After much animated discussion, Sara convinced me to go along to this church one Sunday. Of course, I was looking to add to my growing list of those to hang, so I immediately disliked the young upstart pastor.

When Sara asked about my thoughts, I complained that nobody talked to me. Her sharp but perceptive reply was: 'Of course not. Who wants to talk to someone who has such a black look on his face?' We have always been blunt with each other and she couldn't hide her utter frustration with me.

Then something happened that changed everything. Little Simon came out of Sunday school, beaming. He seemed full of the Holy Spirit and he would not stop talking about Jesus. He was barely three and yet seemed to have grasped all sorts of spiritual concepts, despite living in a household that had mostly stopped talking about the Lord.

I was stunned and deeply moved. The proverbial penny had dropped and I realised that my attitude was extremely unhelpful and could possibly harm my wonderful little family. I was choosing to dwell in the blackest darkness instead of finding my way out into the light.

In parallel to this I had applied for a job in Hong Kong. The salary and the perks were amazing with a hefty bonus at the end of the two-year contract. Like the biblical prophet Jonah, I was running away from my problems, but it felt good. To my mind it all made sense – the company desperately wanted me, our financial situation would be eased, and we had little to lose regarding church and friends here in New Zealand. As such, we accepted, without a moment's thought of the impact it would have on Pop and Lesley.

Sara challenged me that day to ring the pastor and talk out what was niggling me. I did and to my surprise got the associate pastor. We immediately clicked, finding common ground as he had previously lived in Hong Kong. We talked for about an hour as I gingerly opened up about the community, our brush with an assumed cult and my situation.

With a renewed desire to get my life back on track and with the promise of an adventure waiting in Hong Kong, we started going to the church. Of course, my uber-friendly wife made friends straight away while I remained aloof, believing it all to be temporary.

But God had other plans. My boss had broken his leg and was in hospital so when I approached the chief executive at the Fire Service to tell him I was leaving, to my surprise, he panicked. I am not a game player so I was merely informing him, but he came back with a counter-offer. It added 50 per cent to my salary, back pay for all the extra hours I had worked, plus a car for on-call duties and suitable allowances. And if that didn't rock my world, he offered to promote me as a director answering to him and to employ more IT staff.

Things like this only happen once or twice in your life. While considering my options, the Hong Kong job fell through. Well, actually, they just stopped communicating to us about it. As such, I accepted my first role at director level, even though I was barely thirty years old.

It is rare that you find out why God intercepts your carefully considered plans, and changes the course of your life. Usually it remains a mystery. But in this case, a year later I came into contact with one of the twelve kiwis who had accepted a role in Hong Kong. They had sold their house and moved, expecting a wonderful ex-pat life with loads of money. Within months, however, the company had made a strategic decision that forced them to cancel all the contracts and send the kiwis back home with nothing to show for it.

Imagine that; had I run away to Hong Kong as the answer to my financial, business and spiritual woes it would have been a disaster. God spared us from returning months later without a home or job and with another shattered dream weighing down my already burdened soul. The list of those to hang and then forgive would have filled many notebooks.

Instead the Lord intervened. He changed my boss and honoured me through promotion and a massive increase in salary. I was given the use of an office car and paid for being on-call. The need to work ridiculously long hours and weekends was eased by hiring more staff and contracting out some of the tasks. We had also found a place we could call our spiritual home, flawed as it was, and my eldest son had encountered God big-time.

Life had changed course for the better. The cloud was lifted. I hadn't run away and I didn't need to hang people before I had forgiven them. In response to this miracle my diary at the time records this quote taken from Isaiah 26:12: 'All that we have accomplished you have done for us.'

Message to men (MTM)

Next to God Almighty, forgiveness and love are the two most powerful forces in the universe.

If you lack either, you are truly lacking indeed. In fact, you are captive to a sickness of the soul like many of those in the times of Jesus.

Luke 5:18-26 illustrates this point. The sick man lowered through the roof was paralysed, but rather than heal him straight away, Jesus forgave his sin. The Pharisees took offence at Jesus when he dared to forgive the man as they said only God could forgive sins.

Forgiveness is the ultimate in healing. But there are two sides to this coin. We need forgiveness by God, but we also need to forgive others to be set free.

Forgiveness stems from God himself and its application to others is a mandatory requirement to being a true child of the Father. But sometimes we can't forgive others on our own. Like the paralysed man, we need friends to carry us to Jesus.

We see in this story from Luke that forgiveness can help bring healing in our lives. It's not an optional extra. We must be forgiven and forgive to be whole.

Guys, if your soul is poisoned by unforgiveness, then find some friends to help, and together push through until you find yourself at the feet of Jesus. That's when the real miracle begins.

Love prospers when a fault is forgiven …
Proverbs 17:9, NLT

Chapter Twenty-Six
Big and Little Things

World Events

- The break-up of the Soviet Union occurs
- In New Zealand, $1 and $2 notes were discontinued and replaced with coins
- Simon starts school and I find my biological father

'Sometimes,' said Pooh, 'the smallest things take up the most room in your heart.'[42]

The next few years were like that – full of delightful little things. It was good to be back on track rebuilding my faith and dealing with the hurts, where I had a job that was challenging but achievable and was enjoying being a dad to two amazing little lads. And the icing on the cake was that my wonderful wife was also a wonderful mum.

It's true that I was out of my depth being a director, but Sara and I came up with a cunning plan. I would get home from work in good time to be part of the evening routine with the boys. As far as possible, we have always eaten together, relishing the family banter around the dinner table. I would then help bath the boys or shower with them (which was fine until they got to certain height where curiosity became uncomfortable). After that, exhaustion set in so I would let Sara put them to bed as she is a clever story reader. Even today, as the queen of voices, she keeps audiences at the library spellbound during story time.

Once the wee ones were tucked in, I would resume my work, plodding through Everest-sized mountains of paperwork. As a hands-on director, I had little time to cope with the avalanche of written material that stormed my desk each day. Naively, I regarded all of the bulging in-tray as urgent and important so I took the lot home and wouldn't go to bed until I had dealt with it all, only to repeat the same pointless exercise the next night.

Then, one week things changed as my in-tray mysteriously diminished, and stayed that way. About a week later I discovered that it had actually increased so much that it was overflowing into the rubbish bin which was directly underneath it. The five o'clock cleaners were emptying the bin before I had the chance to take it home. Equally baffling was that no one complained, prompting a light-bulb moment for me that those stacks of documents weren't so pressing after all. Over time, I slowly began to triage the urgent from the important by understanding what was a true priority.

My saviour and mentor at the time was a fellow director who had been my temporary boss. Murray was an unlikely father figure, he still acted as if he was a Navy commander barking orders and shouting at staff. His trademark was the smoking of endless roll-your-owns which, in those days, was permitted in the privacy of your own office.

When I visited Murray, I was usually greeted by an angry cloud of smoke and some poor staff member – both eager to escape his office. His mannerisms could be infuriating, but he was also amazingly efficient. At times, I would offload my frustration on him while he chain-smoked and seemed to ignore me. When I finished ranting he would say nothing but merely pass me the pages of a memorandum beautifully laid out with the problem statement, the options and the solution, all done in the few minutes I'd been standing there.

As my coach, Murray said two things to me that had a profound effect on my life, both of which proved not to be true. One day out of the blue, he pronounced, 'You will go far, Lonny, and maybe even make chief executive one day.' While I have been very successful in what I have done, I am glad I have never reached the giddy heights of CEO. Years of observation tell me there is always a high price to it which is usually paid in full at the expense of the family.

However, Murray's words were an inspiration to me, coal to the soul which fired me into action.

The other thing he said was that I couldn't write to save myself. This he loved to say often. Even on my farewell card where he actually said some heart-warming stuff he ended wryly with 'but you still can't write a decent paragraph'. As an author, I sincerely hope this isn't true, but I must confess that writing doesn't come easy. Sentences constantly seem to get in a tangle, but I have two things that allow me to stand tall.

Firstly, Sara is the best copy editor I know, where the words 'critical friend' come to mind. My long-suffering wife bullies my work until it finally reads well or at least makes a modicum of sense. The second thing is my firm belief that the genius is not in the writing, but in the revising. My modus operandi is to energetically type one or two chapters and then spend the rest of the week wrestling with the words until they submit.

Like Pooh, 'My spelling is Wobbly. It's good spelling but it Wobbles, and the letters get in the wrong places.'[43] This can be disastrous.

Another event that involved little things was Sara's thirtieth birthday. We organised a high tea for her friends and arranged that they could come to our house unencumbered by children. I took the day off and we used Sue's house for me to oversee the tiny tots gleefully offloaded by eager mums who hurried next door to play ladies. For me it was a small thing to do as I loved babies then as I do now, but my wife remembers it as one of the biggest acts of kindness in our marriage.

In the summer of 1991, I used my holiday leave to paint our house. Once the disgusting job of sanding and preparing the weatherboards was done there was no end of volunteers to splash paint about as Simon and Nat were very keen to help their daddy. Being a bit of a perfectionist, I had to choose their tasks well. Obviously, the ladders and trestles were out of the question so I convinced Sara to paint the gate with them while I did the high stuff.

Etched in my mind is a picture of Simon diligently painting, with his tongue hanging out, while Nat spent most of his time juggling a brush which kept falling into the bucket of paint. Nonplussed, Nat would plunge into the bucket, lift out the saturated brush and splosh about trying to imitate his big brother. Sara eventually noticed this repeated mishap and exclaimed, 'Be careful with your brush, Natty.' Unfortunately, she was on her knees painting a low bit of the fence right next to him. His reply, 'What, Mummy?' as he swivelled around ended with him painting her entire face with the dripping brush. I nearly fell off the ladder laughing.

At this time we also began to take pre-marriage courses. Out of desperation, our pastor had developed his own material as nothing suitable seemed to exist. After taking several courses, we thought little of how hard this could be as they seemed to go swimmingly.

However, small things can cast big shadows. During one session with two fairly new Christians everything blew up. We were innocently covering the topic on forgiveness of past wrongs, and had mentioned in passing previous sexual encounters. The husband-to-be was open and frank about his experiences but naively assumed his wife-to-be was a virgin. When she confessed otherwise he went nuts.

After several minutes of ranting and rage it was obvious that somehow, he perceived that it was alright for him to have had a sexual past but not for her. By implication he implied that men could be forgiven such behaviour but women could not. Needless to say, they never completed the course – they couldn't while he was married to the past.

Some truly cool things happened that year which weren't so small. While at work one day I got a phone call to say I had won a trip. Unbeknown to me, every time I had bought computer consumables I had entered into a draw. The prize was a trip for two to Melbourne to see *The Phantom of the Opera* with luxury accommodation, $500 spending money and limousine transport to and from the show.

Everything about the trip was marvellous, no small detail overlooked. The musical was enchanting and the hotel had a marble bathroom where we thoroughly enjoyed soaking in the large bath. Melbourne was a paradise for places to eat and with prize money begging to be spent, we made the most of it. We both came back home a little larger than when we left – me, because of my indulgence in fantastic Greek food, and Sara because she had become pregnant.

In spring that year, Simon started school. I had been advised to take the day off, not so much for Simon but for Sara. The lad was used to being at school as he had spent many afternoons with his grandma, who taught new entrants, and he fitted in really well. Sure enough, on the day he started school he waved us goodbye and forgot about us as soon as he walked into the classroom.

Sara, on the other hand, was tearful and sad. This day can be momentous for the primary caregiver, there is a letting go and a sense of loss when you hand your first child over to the school system. We went out for coffee and chatted for a while before we had to get back to the young Nat-Man.

There was other grieving that happened this year. The young preacher had left the church soon after I became an elder, and so had the associate pastor who was seeking to be an overseas missionary. The church had voted in the part-time pastor, an older man who was not theologically trained. Just after taking office his teenage son was killed by a car.

As is so often the case when one life ends another starts; on the day of the funeral we confirmed that Sara was pregnant. I remember Sara and her friend Heather both whispering their good news to each other while trying not to disrupt the solemn atmosphere.

The previous year Sara's only aunty living in New Zealand had come down to Wellington for Buncle's wedding (Sara's brother is also called Simon so to avoid confusion with two Simons in the family, we called him Big Uncle Simon. Since it was a mouthful for the kids we shortened Big Uncle Simon to Big Uncle and then shrunk it even further to Buncle and now Bunc).

As a seasoned Mormon, Sara's aunty knew all the tricks of the trade for tracking down ancestors and with Sara's encouragement she taught her about researching genealogy. Sara then used this knowledge to find my biological father.

All my life I had been told that he had been taken away by the police after trying to kill us children (although I never believed it). The story goes that Mum had made him a coffee cake for his birthday and as he held the knife to cut it, something snapped. He could no longer bear the responsibility of fatherhood so with knife in hand he advanced on our bedrooms to end the life of his three small boys. Mum stood in the way and was stabbed just as my uncle arrived home to wrestle the knife from my father. The authorities then locked him away in a psychiatric ward and threw away the key.

The story sounds utterly bizarre and if it wasn't for the fact that my mother also told Sara, who wrote it down, I would have doubted I had heard it right.

After much searching, Sara found Lionel and, you guessed it, he wasn't insane, he wasn't an attempted murderer – just a sick man confined to the house. The story was fabricated purely to protect my mother's indiscretions which my father had somehow stumbled upon.

Hoping that I could find some closure, and fill the empty hole inside that had gnawed at me for so long, we tentatively made contact with Lionel. Growing up I had secretly romanticised my absent father into some great man who was desperately looking for his children but couldn't find them as my wicked mother had remarried and hidden our identities.

My first shock was that he didn't want to see me. When I persisted in writing to him, my second shock was that he denied being my father, telling me to talk to my mother about it. This had a ring of truth to it as indeed my elder brother was not his child. Lionel had been duped into marrying my mother on the pretext that she was pregnant to him. I, however, was truly his son, as was my younger brother. You only had to look at us to see the close resemblance.

Eventually, he agreed to meet us. The third shock came when we flew to Christchurch, only to have his wife refuse to let us past the front door. We politely stood our ground unwilling to budge until Lionel intervened and demanded that she let us in. The final shock to me was that they were incredibly poor, they nailed blankets up for curtains and used duct tape around the windows to stop the draughts. There was little furniture apart from a stereo that he had bought with some inheritance money.

I was only two years old when he had left. I was so small but I was not a thing that took up most of the room in his heart. My childhood daydreams were shattered that year. Still, there were plenty of positives to make up for it, especially with the excitement of having another baby to add to our delightful family. I couldn't wait to meet this little person who I just knew would steal my heart. And I wasn't disappointed. 'We'll be friends until forever, just you wait and see.'[44]

Message to men (MTM)

My childhood was far from perfect. Life hadn't been good to me back then, but as an adult I had clear choice. I could carry the darkness I experienced as a boy into fatherhood, or I could learn to love and, with the help of a gracious God, be better for it.

William L. Watkinson once said as part of a sermon in 1907 that it is 'far better to light the candle than to curse the darkness'.[45]

When things are pressing in on you, overwhelming you, a candle doesn't seem like much. But choosing not to be negative, and to find the good using what little light you have, can make all the difference to your life.

Combine this with a deep appreciation for the small things in life and you have a recipe for joy, despite the odds.

Marriage can become dull when we lose our fire as men. But here's the thing: it's not the big things that cause this, it's the lack of all the tiny joys you once had together.

Be determined to rekindle those things. It may be listening to music while cuddling on the couch, going for a walk and talk, breakfast in bed together, meeting up and having a quick beer after work, cooking dates, gardening together, planning holidays – taking holidays. If you take a moment to reflect on what was once fun in your relationship, I'm sure your list would be endless.

We blokes need to grasp these two liberating thoughts and carve them deep into our thick skulls – small things matter and you are not the product of your circumstances.

When faced with dark times you can either curse life or you can be a light through living God's way.

> *A simple life in the Fear-of-God is better than a rich life*
> *with a ton of headaches.*
> Proverbs 15:16, *The Message*

Chapter Twenty-Seven
What's in a Gift?

World Events
- After a public outcry over royal spending, the Queen of England volunteers to pay income tax for the first time
- Tiny New Zealand voted on to the UN Security Council
- Sara highly pregnant with our third child

Winston Churchill is sometimes quoted as saying: 'We make a living by what we get. We make a life by what we give.'[46] My take on this is that giving is the active ingredient in a good marriage. It is love at its best. But giving can easily be misapplied and misguided.

Twenty-six years ago our financial state was all over the place. Supporting a growing family and maintaining an old house will always be a money pit, but at least our savings were heading in the right direction.

The windfall of unattached cash that occasionally blew my way allowed me to play the romantic. In those days, without the insight of Gary Chapman's 'love languages', I thought that buying gifts was how you expressed love. However, I was to discover that some gifts are, as they say, as useful as a cat flap on a submarine.

The intention was always good but the delivery sometimes fell short. The list of Carey family legends is stacked with exaggerated stories of misfires when it comes to hitting the good gifts target.

As a try-hard romantic I was always on the lookout for opportunities to spoil my beloved. One time, Sara complained of having achy feet. That information was tucked away and when Christmas rolled around I triumphantly gave her a relaxing foot-spa. But she didn't find it at all soothing – she hated the fuss of having to get towels, fill it with warm water and add various bath salts when all she fancied was for her dim-witted husband to gently rub her feet at the end of each day.

The ebb and flow of bad gifts had started years earlier when on my birthday I was presented with a coffee table that she had admired for some time. To justify the purchase, she had asked Pop to paint a chessboard on the glass especially for me. But I wasn't fooled and as soon as I opened the present I mentally added that one to the legendary misfires list. Another time, I bought two pairs of earrings while overseas and gave the set of pretty parrots to Lesley. The life lesson there was to let your wife choose first; more than twenty years later she still reminds me of that misdemeanour. Things aren't helped when a gloating Lesley parades around with them dangling from her lobes, purposefully eliciting a response from Sara.

As a word of caution, it is easy to be critical of gifts but it is dangerous to disapprove of your wife's judgement. After all, just look at who she married.

The gentle art of giving and receiving requires much grace and a selfless focus on the other person's desires. Sometimes, you just need to be generous-hearted and overlook misguided gifts – that's what lovers do. At other times, you need to make a stand, and on one occasion Sara bought clothes as Nat's presents. As the saying goes, there is nothing as miserable as giving a young child what they need for Christmas.[48] Knowing this, I intervened and added a toy bank truck that had a slot in the roof for money. She argued that he had plenty of cars and trucks and that another one was wasteful. My counter to this was based on years of feeling utterly deflated when I opened yet more socks and undies from my mother at Christmas.

The victory belongs to the truck as Nat not only loved it on sight, it has remained a favourite toy throughout the years. Somehow this love has been passed down through the genes as my grandson Levi adores that battered old red truck when he comes to play at Grandad's.

The worse example of a present gone wrong has to be from the husband of good friends at the time. Soon after Christmas we had dinner together, only to discover that his present to her had been a large six-burner barbecue. Intrigued, I chatted to him over a beer or two while he barbecued our food on her shiny new toy. He just couldn't understand why she was so cross and hadn't spoken to him since Christmas Day.

Knowing how your spouse is wired plays an important part in getting gifts right. However, physical gifts are only a small piece in the jigsaw of giving. A great marriage is full of love where the husband and a wife are giving to each other on many different planes. The giving of oneself to each other is the heart of a successful marriage.

It took me many battle-weary years to realise that Sara's love language was not gifts but giving. It sometimes made her cross when I gave her unnecessary gifts, especially if finances were tight.

The best gift for my Sara is performing acts of kindness. Looking out for how I can help or what I can do for her far outweighs a trunk full of trinkets that she doesn't want or need. But that's not to say all gifts are unwanted.

One Valentine's Day while she was teaching, I sent a large bunch of beautiful roses to her school. She was walking back from swimming with her juniors when one of the big kids appeared with the flowers. Many eyes saw the delight on her face which quickly became the talk of the school. She glowed for days after that, but it was my thoughtfulness rather than the flowers that had mattered the most to her.

Our tenth wedding anniversary underlined this point. We saved for ages so we could go somewhere posh for dinner. The evening was really special, more so because in 1990 it was very difficult to find anything open on New Year's Day. Anyway, I wanted to spoil my sweetheart by buying her ten red roses as well, but the problem was that we just did not have any money to spare.

So Mr Creative came up with an idea. Using a red vivid marker, I drew ten rose buds on a sheet of clean computer paper, the kind with the holes down the sides. And amazingly she loved them, so much so that she has kept them for over a quarter of a century and still proudly pulls the sheet out during the marriage courses we run. In her words, 'I still have those roses in my drawer and I remember that anniversary very fondly because of the silliness and the effort he put into those flowers!'

Despite being an aspiring romantic, I still got it slightly wrong because I thought Sara loved red roses. It's the truth, she loves roses but it wasn't until decades later I discovered her favourite is actually yellow.

However, the one gift I know that is sure-fire is shoes. As I said earlier, Sara is passionate about shoes. Her eyes widen when we pass a shoe shop which, when combined with the magnetic force of the word 'sale', seems to suck her in with the power of an interstellar supernova. My wife must be related to Bette Midler who allegedly once said, 'Give a girl the right shoes, and she can conquer the world.'[49]

Ages ago, I sneakily drew an outline of her shoes and then saved some money from various discrete sources so I could buy her her first pair of expensive trainers. Back then the cost was scary so I locked them away in the work safe until her birthday. On the grand day when she opened her present her eyes nearly popped out of her head. Just feeling that the gift was in a shoebox was enough to get her adrenaline pumping.

Despite having periods of misunderstanding each other's love languages, often through my overemphasis on tangible gifts, when we knew what made each other tick it became easy for me to express kind actions to Sara.

What was confusing to me, how to please my wife, is now simple – knowing that she is about to come home I will have the table set and the dishes in the sink cleared away, maybe a glass of wine poured and music playing in the background to accompany the delicious dinner I have cooked.

For someone whose primary love language is kind actions, every time you do something thoughtful for them you give them a clear signal that you are thinking of them, that they matter to you, that they are your top priority in a crazy, busy life. For them it's the action that matters above all else and if these types of things aren't done then gifts are trivialised – somewhat like annoying loose change rattling around in your pocket compared to $100 notes neatly folded in your wallet.

Life is wonderful a gift from God. Each year Sara and I enjoy together:

365 sunrises
1,100 meals
5.8 million words spoken
7.3 million breaths
42 million heartbeats

And I know that the Lord is the sustainer of them all.

Message to men (MTM)

Men, let's look at the gift of listening to your wife. If we are honest, listening is seldom a strong point for men.

Before you laugh it off, it's actually a big deal. Most women would rather spend time with someone who listens to them than have sex. In fact, it is often an underlying cause of relationship failures.

Turn to social media or psychology articles and you will see them laden with complaints about blokes being poor listeners.

Typically, we men would rather avoid long conversations about feelings or endless trivia or about problems that we know how to solve but where she doesn't want to know the answers.

Surveys claim that men average just six minutes of listening to their partners before they switch off. And yet, we can concentrate at work for hours during meetings, or focus on other blokes at a barbecue rambling on about sport.

What a gift we can give our wives by actively listening without judgement or interruption. What a simple way to enrich our marriages and be a better person for it. What an easy win that reaps big rewards.

As a couple, listening is a great tool for bringing us closer to each other. When we are in tune with each other, everything seems right with the world.

Gary Chapman nails it in his book *Everybody Wins* when he says, 'Don't talk, listen to her. Her thoughts are trapped inside her and they need to get out and you are her escape. Are we truly listening or just using the time to reload our verbal guns?'[50]

> *To answer before listening – that is folly and shame.*
> Proverbs 18:13

Chapter Twenty-Eight
Abscrabscarey

World Events

- Prince Charles and Princess Diana separate
- South Africans vote to end apartheid
- Student loans introduced in NZ clocking up a billion dollars per year in debt
- Abi Carey is born

One of the greatest gifts I have ever received was that of my darling daughter. All my children were like sunshine for my soul. I have known great joy being the father of three little ones, but it was a surprise to me that being a parent could be so much fun.

In the midst of all the chaos, things can seem very different. Every mother and father of young children know that parenting is an impossible challenge – there is never enough time, energy, or spare pairs of hands; money and sleep are always scarce and good sex becomes but a vague memory. With so many chores and things to wrestle with, life can feel like it is on repeat.

One stage of growth rumbles into another with a relentless barrage of new demands needing your attention. And yet parenting can be deeply satisfying. The birth of Abi in 1992 completed my little family and so began the adventure of fulfilling my life's ambition to break the mould and live as a family for God.

The previous year my younger brother, Vic, surprised the Carey tribe by having a baby girl. Until then there had been a succession of twelve boys born without the slightest hint of a female joining the family except through marriage.

I had secretly wanted a daughter, but growing up in a household of raucous lads left me unsure how I would cope and Sara had certainly proven that girls were a mystery to me. Little did I know there is a special bond that exists between a father and a daughter in a way that is different to boys.

Until my daughter was born I had been an elder in the church by popular vote. And I hated it. Politics in a democratic church is something to behold. Our church at the time included founding members who had helped build the structure but not the church. They only showed their faces when it came to formal church meetings so they could cast their votes.

Every time we attended one of these meetings someone would nudge me in the back when the subject of eldership came up. Maybe it was that I seemed a model candidate with a good-looking wife and beautiful young family and I spoke my mind.

Eventually, after some token prayer, I caved in and to my surprise was elected as an elder. And I immediately regretted it. The qualities required for an elder in the church were scarily elastic. The role was far more politician than elder, and I soon discovered that the way I am wired does not conduct the current of game playing.

But popular vote doesn't cut it with God or my wife. As Billy Sunday allegedly said, 'Your reputation is what people say about you. Your character is what God and your wife know about you.'[51]

Marriage has this wonderful trait of being a reality check. Sara knew that my faith at the time was somewhat like James Bond's favourite drink – it was dry and shaken but not stirred. I was slowly retaking ground that I had once claimed, but I was also deeply weary.

As such, we began to question whether I done the right thing and when Sara became pregnant again I took the opportunity to resign from eldership on the grounds that I wanted more time to focus on my new baby. And I am glad that I did.

Sara's third pregnancy went well, but we were constantly on edge. After the last lightning deliveries, the midwife had prepared a home kit for us in the form of a long rolled-up towel and rubber sheet with other things tucked in between. In the last trimester we clung to it like a security blanket, taking it wherever we went. But life always has the last laugh and on the night of Abi's birth, things happened as if they were scripted from a textbook.

Labour started in earnest around bedtime for Simon and Nat. When Sara casually mentioned that she was in labour, I immediately wanted to speed to the hospital with all lights blazing. My calm wife had other ideas as she wished to see the end of *Coronation Street* on TV (which ironically she has never watched again). As it was, we rang the midwife and Lesley and then sat down for half an hour of soapy entertainment. We then moseyed down the road and checked in to the maternity ward. In a couple of hours, this time with Lesley present, Abigail Carey was born. The birth was uneventful and then she was with us, in the delivery room and in my heart forever. I was punch-drunk with shock that I had a daughter.

As with all my children I was immediately in love with her, in an unreserved and besotted way. Abi screamed for four hours after being born, which was the first hint of her feisty character. Within a short while she earned herself the well-deserved nickname of Abscrabscarey.

Unfortunately, as a newborn her low time corresponded with Sara's. I often came home from work to find Sara juggling a restless baby in one arm while trying to cook dinner with the other. The routine quickly became that I would take the baby and feed her a bottle while we watched the news together. It was hard on Sara waiting until saviour Daddy strode in through the door, but I loved it. Through these intimate times I developed a very special bond with my daughter.

As parents of two easy-going boys, we thought we had it sussed – we could have written the textbook on child-rearing. Then along came number three, a girl with a frighteningly similar personality to her spirited mother. This insight became all too clear when Abi was a teenager and the two ladies in the house were at odds with each other. Commenting on how alike they were back then was like pouring petrol on a smouldering bonfire. Both of them would turn the full blast of their fiery personalities onto the poor hapless person who had dared to mention it. Nowadays, they both laugh and nod sagely, acknowledging the truth of it.

From the day when she was first able to express herself, Abi let us know that she never wanted to be the youngest. She wished to do everything her older brothers were doing. Worse still, she wanted to be the big sister who bossed everyone else around. Despite the six years' difference in age, it was not uncommon for her to punch Simon full in the stomach in frustration. Luckily, he was big enough and kind enough to laugh it off. Nat, on the other hand, was fairer game. The rivalry between the two was often hilarious as Abi quickly learned that she could get Nat into trouble for hitting her even when he wasn't in the same room.

Like a lot of daughters, Abi adopted an attitude of, 'My fingers may be small but I can still wrap Dad around them.' This worked to a degree, but Sara and I had strategies.

Children are naturally manipulative. How else do they survive in a world dominated by big people? One of the best apparatuses in our parenting toolkit was being united in front of the children. If we disagreed, it was a private discussion later. A clever child will take on one parent, like a lion isolating its prey, but few have the courage to charge the determined herd of adults.

Of course, both parents are not always around at the same time. As our kids got older we insisted, where possible, that we were given a chance to confer before decisions were made, to avoid the divide and conquer tactic that all children come equipped with. This got us both into hot water in Abi's later teenage years when we were accused of not having minds of our own, or of being dominated by the other parent, or simply being weak. However, it was extremely effective, much to the frustration of the offended party.

Once the boundaries were there and clear, there was much freedom in-between. It never ceased to amaze me that all three children could go across the road to their grandparents (who had moved to be closer), and experience a completely different set of family rules – happily adjusting without any fuss.

The approach of being clear and consistent had its rewards as parents, leaving us with many very happy memories.

I realised early on that the strains on a young mum were huge and that Sara needed not just a helping hand but genuine breaks.

It's fair to say I was adventurous as a dad of young ones, although a little misguided at times. Once, I glibly sent Sara away on a road trip with her mum for a well-deserved break. Abi was only just walking at the time. That Sunday morning, I got all three dressed and fed and then dressed again to remove the breakfast spatters. We arrived at church with me proudly parading them through the door as the sole-charge superdad when one of the mums quickly took me aside to tell me that Abi's pinafore was on back to front. Being adventurous is one thing, being competent is another.

One of the nicest sets of memories I have is of my daddy-daughter dates. I would try to have one-on-one time with each of the kids once in a while. It was their time so, within reason, they got to say what we did. With Abi, it was usually something like going to a movie and having a hot chocolate with marshmallows in a posh café afterwards.

We still have these dates as adults where they usually include a meal out together. We love going to the movies and often enjoy the banter of trying to match quotes with the right film.

But it wasn't all fun. There were times where I nearly missed my daughter's life – times later on while we were living in England when I did not get home until her bedtime, and really only saw her at weekends.

Each of these times caused deep angst inside me and eventually I would take drastic action to ensure I was part of her life again. This involved things like returning to New Zealand for the lifestyle, or taking up skiing as a common hobby, and collecting DVDs so we could watch them together during family times each Friday night.

My daughter has always been spirited and definitely knows her own mind, but she has also grown to be a wonderfully generous woman who is very kind and loads of fun to be around. She has taught me a lot.

I have always believed that getting married was God's greatest training ground for me. I am a prince of heaven solely by the actions of Jesus but while on earth, my Father is schooling me to become a real man who knows how to love.

Marriage and raising children are avenues of growth, reflecting and refining who we truly are, but they are also wonderful opportunities to experience the full impact of love as it was meant to be. And love is the joy of life.

Message to men (MTM)

OK, it's time for some advice on the tricky subject of daughters.

Firstly, I know from observation and personal experience that daughters have a unique bond with their dads and that fathers have a powerful influence over them in a way that is different to mothers. In a sense, you are her first love.

From a young age, your daughter will look to you for reassurance that you think she is both beautiful and smart. She will crave your attention – so tune in to her and connect with her. Make time for her daily and remember those all-important daddy-daughter dates.

Fathers have an incredible sway over their daughter's future relationship. From birth she is watching how you treat her mother. So be the man you would want her to marry, and take care to role model a loving relationship with your wife that is based on mutual respect.

Set healthy boundaries because she needs your protection. This can be difficult when your daughter is a teenager as often she believes that Mum is constantly preaching at her and she will try to manipulate you by playing the 'trust me' card. But boundaries aren't about trust, they are safety fences that we all need, especially teenagers. On this point you need to stay firm and united. Later on, she will thank you both for it.

Lastly, your daughter sees you as a hero. So be one to her. Fight for her soul. Show her by your lifestyle, your resolve, and your love that a relationship with God is everything she could ever desire.

Charm is deceptive, and beauty is fleeting, but a woman [daughter] who fears the Lord is to be praised.
Proverbs 31:30

Chapter Twenty-Nine
Strange Love

World Events
- World Trade Center bombed
- First cloned cells from human embryos
- Prior to 1993 women were not allowed to wear trousers on the US Senate floor
- My nanna and grandad died the year before

We now live in a society where it is legally easier and less risky to dump your wife than to fire an employee.
Maggie Gallagher[52]

Some say that love is strange. I would go so far as to say that human love is the Frankenstein of all emotions. In a bizarre twist to the monster in the movies, much of what passes as love today appears attractive on the outside whereas a brute so often lurks within.

Love's Frankenstein is a concoction of Hollywood romance mixed with the young and the beautiful stitched together by casual sex and hasty decisions. It may appear free and inviting, but its true nature sees others as objects where its ugliness is clothed in a thin layer of attractive but fleeting emotion. When the feelings subside, the lover is cast aside and the beast moves on to its next victim.

The best example of strange love I know is that of my grandparents. Despite there being many reasons to the contrary, they gave the impression they were devoted to each other. One of these contrary indications happened on their fiftieth wedding anniversary. On that auspicious day, my grandparents announced to the remaining nine of their ten children that they were fathered from two brothers. It seemed that my nana had had a long-standing affair with Grandad's brother. I vividly recall the event as all hell broke out. The celebration turned into a monster-hunt with torches brightly ablaze revealing an angry mob out for blood.

Grandad was no saint, but he was a character. He loved his whisky and nothing pleased him more than mixing his drinking with horse racing. This toxic combination caught up with him one day. After a successful day of punting on the gee-gees and drinking away the profits, he was involved in a nasty car accident. The vehicle was a write-off but Grandad, in his overly relaxed state, was unharmed. When he climbed out of the wreck to abuse the other driver, he was surprised to find that the offending party was in fact a parked car.

I was a teenager at the time and was often the recipient of a phone call from Grandad after a day's heavy drinking and betting. He would shout down the phone for someone to come to pick him up at 'Me Aunties' (the pub was at a placed called Meeanee). Since he was partly deaf he couldn't hear the person on the other end of the telephone, so he would just hang up expecting a driver to appear pronto.

Nana was a sweeter soul, who would bike around to our place once a week. She liked to get out and about, which was probably a good thing as their house usually had all the curtains pulled and the doors and windows firmly shut. Since they lived in one of New Zealand's hotter climates this meant the house smelt terribly of musty old people. For some reason Nana and Grandad called my mum Sis. After the night of horror when they announced how they had created their unnatural family, I dared not ask why she was nicknamed Sis.

I recall Nana and Grandad arguing a lot, especially one time when Sara and I naively asked them questions about their family line during the phase of our lives when Sara was attempting to make sense of my past. At that time we had just proudly presented baby Simon as their great-grandson. But instead of this being a moment of joy and elation like heralding the arrival of Simba on Pride Rock,[53] they totally ignored him.

We then moved on to asking about the past. In my family, questions like that can be the lightning rod that brings the monster to life. Eventually we left them to their bickering, disappointed at a lack of interest that had spanned a lifetime for me.

A few years later, in 1993, my nana passed away. When I arrived for the funeral I found my grandad deeply sad. What I had seen on the surface was but a mere sliver of the truth regarding their marriage, but what I do know now is that he found it impossible to live without his wife. Six months later he died from what I suspect was a broken heart. Their love was strange and twisted, not formed from the usual body of companionship, faithfulness or respect, but rather through a powerful chemistry that had existed over a long period of time.

My stepfather, Tom, also had a strange but unwavering love for them. Despite my mum divorcing him and remarrying twice over, he remained loyal to her parents who lived in the same city. He would pop around to see them and do odd jobs when needed. When it came to the cost of two funerals in quick session, my mother asked Tom if he would contribute, which he did without hesitation.

Years later when Tom and I were visiting Mum's grave, he proudly told me that he came without fail every Saturday. While he was at the graveyard he would pay a visit to my grandparents' plot and keep it tidy. Intrigued, I went with my stepdad to see their headstone and discovered that for well over a decade he had been carefully tending someone else's site. Since he couldn't read, he had relied on his usually dependable memory which in this case had sadly let him down.

Instead of taking it to heart, my matter-of-fact stepdad just cursed and we set off looking for the right spot. Nana and Grandad were not particularly nice to Dad, treating him as if he was deaf and dumb and never good enough for Sis. My mum had dumped him long ago, but still he remained unmoving in his devotion to them all.

Real love is a choice you make over and over again. It is not some twisted emotion – here today all bright and beautiful, gone tomorrow striding off into the dark. My stepfather is a man of honour who chose to love despite the lack of returned affection.

I was moved to find that he went to the graveyard every week to do what he could for deceased people who had treated him unkindly. He held no grudges and only saw the best in them. When you look beyond his rough exterior, my lovely Dad is the rare find, a heart of gold.

Mary Shelley, in her book, quotes Frankenstein's creation as saying, 'There is love in me the likes of which you've never seen. There is rage in me the likes of which should never escape. If I am not satisfied in the one, I will indulge the other.'[54]

There is a fraudulent form of love that rages within us that deceives us into placing our belief in the great pretender the world calls love. Like my dad, we need to choose wisely and indulge in the kind of pure love our Lord Jesus modelled.

For many people, the love of God is strange, but for Sara and me it is our reason for living. Unlike Dr Frankenstein, our creator loves us and does not shun us as ugly beasts. His love is not strange because he sees us as his beautiful children with the extravagant love of a doting father.

Message to men (MTM)

This chapter is about radical thinking, especially regarding the subject of love. Just how different is kingdom thinking? For example, do you really believe the Bible is the Word of God and is infallible?

Let's take two versions of the Beatitudes found in Luke 6:20-22 to test how profound the teaching of Jesus is and how far our modern Christian minds have distorted these truths.

1. 'Blessed are you who are poor, for yours is the kingdom of God.'
   Blessed are the well-off, for they have many resources that can be used for the kingdom of God.

2. 'Blessed are you who hunger now, for you will be satisfied.'
   Blessed are you who are satisfied with many good things, for you aren't distracted by needing much.

3. 'Blessed are you who weep now, for you will laugh.'
   Blessed are you who are emotionally balanced, so people will look to you as having your life together.

4. 'Blessed are you when people hate you, when they exclude you and insult you and reject your name as evil, because of the Son of Man.'
   Blessed are you who get on well with everyone and are well-connected, for the favour of men will be used for the kingdom's sake.

Which version do you relate to? Now, consider again this well-known proverb:

> *Trust in the Lord with all your heart and*
> *lean not on your own understanding …*
> Proverbs 3:5

Chapter Thirty
Chapter to Myself

Yesterday I was clever, so I wanted to change the world.
Today I am wise, so I am changing myself.
Jalaluddin Rumi[55]

A conversation between my younger (in italics) and older selves.

Let's talk about marriage.
What's there to talk about? I am madly in love and we have our whole married life in front of us.

How about we discuss all the things I did well in the marriage and a few not-so-great things I wish I knew about so I could avoid them early on?
Sounds intriguing. Hit me with it.

Hmm. Number one on the list is to respect older people. Not because they are your elders (as if that gives them some superior right), but actually because they know a thing or two.
Like what? They often seem so negative. I sometimes feel like they are judging me, especially now that we have little kids.

What older people have that you don't have is years of living. They each have a story to tell – they have life lessons waiting to explode out into the open if only people were interested. Young people have always turned to their mates for advice as their first port of call, but God's order is that the old teach the young.

Are you saying that we should discuss marriage problems with our parents? Surely that's a step too far; parents would naturally side with their own child.

I see you have wisdom. Yes and no is the answer. By all means, where you both agree and where it would be helpful, talk to your parents about your marriage. You will be amazed at what they know and what they have been through. However, if it's a sticky topic someone more independent is better by far. My advice is to foster some solid relationships with older couples in the church. They don't have to be perfect, but you both need to respect them.

That's really difficult to achieve. There is hardly enough time in the week for just the two of us. Even squeezing in friends is a challenge except when all the kids are present. How can we find time to get to know older couples? Life is just too busy.

I hear you. The period when your children are little often collides with an accelerating career and fending off increasing demands in the church. It seems everyone wants a 'piece' of you.

Spot on. So why would I add to my pressures? Isn't it better to reserve time for my wife?

Yes, that is very important. But a relationship with someone is a living thing. When it is first born, it is vulnerable like a

baby, needing constant attention, but to really mature it must have support from those much older than itself. Imagine a world where children brought each other up.
You have my attention, go on…

This is where older people come in. Be creative to make time for them. It could be you ask them to babysit and then deliberately spend thirty minutes at the end chatting about things before they go home. Or you can include them in holiday plans. Maybe it's a coffee once a month, or breakfast. Your relationship can only benefit and grow when given loving and wise guidance.
OK, got it… What next?

There is one thing I wish I had been better at in my marriage and that is to really cherish my wife.
But I adore her. She's the light of my life. Things couldn't be better. We are both totally in love.

Yes, but do you really cherish her? It's the one thing the Lord kept telling me to do over and over.
What do you mean? Can you elaborate?

Do you argue, sometimes viciously, over hot topics that you can't recall just a few days later? Do you pout and sulk when things aren't going your way? Do you have mean thoughts about her, sometimes for days on end?
Alright, enough, I get the point. I'm not perfect and you are being judgemental. What's this got to do with cherishing her?

Forgive me, I'm just making a point. To really cherish her is to see the best in her when there is doubt. Often our minds leap to conclusions without knowing all the facts. It's as simple as cutting through the fog of emotion and negativity to see her point of view. But that takes active and intentional listening. How do you rate yourself in the listening stakes?

Not great, I guess. I often can't remember things almost as soon as I am told them. I seem to filter out the stuff I think is unimportant and jump into solution mode.

Listening well is one of strongest acts of love there is. It shows you are connecting with her heart and not just her mind. She feels understood and appreciates that you are trying to see the real person. Solution mode is often belittling if it is not seasoned with a heavy dose of empathy.

Interesting. So what else?

Well, cherishing her also means paying her constant attention. It truly is the little things that count over the long-term. Those gentle acts of courtesy by opening a door, telling her she is gorgeous, brushing pass her deliberately, texts over how her day is going, loving it when she does things for you, not being afraid to hold her hand in public, praising her in front of others. All these and hundreds more all add to your beloved feeling like she is your queen and not just in name only.

I heard once that a man told his wife that he loved her on their wedding day and that he would let her know if anything changed.

Ouch! I have made a habit of telling Sara that I love her as we go to sleep. It's a nice way to end the day and just one more token into the bank account of love.

Can we talk for a bit about arguing? We argue a lot. She is a quicker thinker than me and always seems to challenge my leadership with annoying alternatives. I often feel undermined.

Let's cover some of the basics I have learned the hard way. You mentioned parents taking sides. Never go to them about an argument. It will naturally polarise them, and your wife will feel utterly betrayed. Next, learn to argue well.

Now, that sounds crazy. Surely those two words are contradictory.

Arguments are a key tool to moving into new plains of understanding. Without hearty discussion things simmer and like a slow poison will eventually contaminate your relationship. However, arguments can also be very destructive. Things said and done in anger are remembered long after the issue is forgotten.

That's the truth. How can we avoid such carnage?

Some simple rules are needed to override your emotion at the time. Whole books and seminars are based on this, but the point is to stick with the issue. Attack the problem together, not the person.

It all sounds so easy, but how?

Obviously don't name call – that's about the person, not the issue. Then use non-inflammatory language to describe your feelings and how things are affecting you. Next take a deep breath – a deliberate pause – and then open your ears wider than your mouth.

Ha ha, I like that.

You will be surprised once you express yourself and then listen well without trying to win the argument. Much of the heat of the moment is due to miscommunication. Once you know her side and that she actually intended no harm, things cool fast.

Ah, and then there are the loving feelings that come – making up can be so much fun.

You're onto it. Cherishing her means seeing the best in her even when you are wounded and suspect she has mistreated you.

Like those well-known verses in 1 Corinthians 13. Love 'is not easily angered' and 'keeps no record of wrongs'.

One last thing. Always stay teachable and laugh lots, especially at yourself.

I'm not so great at that. In fact, if I make a mistake or embarrass myself, I dwell on it for days, especially if she laughs at me.

She is laughing with you out of kindness – not at you like you are an idiot.
It doesn't always feel that way. It hurts.

It hurts because you are striving to impress and for perfection. Making mistakes is what makes us humans and not little gods. The thing is not to let mistakes destroy you but to have resilience – brush them off with a hearty laugh and then learn from what happened. See them as a positive. My lovely wife describes them as mere bumps in the road.
You say God constantly told you to cherish your wife. Why did he have to tell you so many times?

There were issues that just never died, they seemed to resurface in a slightly different form. Like the hydra monster, it seemed that when we cut off one head another slightly different one grew in its place.
Now you have my attention. Please go on.

This is one thing you have to figure out for yourself and together with our wife. I am referring of course to the physical side of your marriage. The chalk and cheese, the hot and cold, the Mars and Venus contrasts where deeply ingrained differences exist.
I get what you mean. But how do we solve this?

You don't. But by genuine appreciation of each other you can make great strides. For you it is about understanding her need to connect first, to feel safe and to have a degree of control. It is about being loved and not about the act of sex.
I know all that, but so often it feels like a battle, like I am constantly the one who is thinking of her in this way but without it being reciprocated.

That's the hydra monster for you. Good love-making is only the tip of the iceberg of a deeply satisfying relationship.
Now you are being poetic rather than helpful. Again, how do I solve this?

You are in solution mode again. As I said, cherish her above all else. Make sure the balance of listening is always in her favour. Forgo the physical and focus on connecting with her as a person.
That sounds like it will take too much time to get anywhere near success.

Forget success and go for significance. Take the pressure right off and you may be surprised by how she reacts. Again, things won't change overnight as she will be deeply suspicious of your motives, but in time as she begins to see you are more interested in her than her body, she will respond well.
But it's always me that has to initiate things. I am a quality time person – that is my love language, I hate the 'get it over with' attitude I detect at times.

You need to grow some! I mean patience and insight. Set aside special date nights to ensure you have quality times, talk to her about things, laugh a lot, keep it fun and make it pleasurable for you both. What woman wouldn't want that? *True, I guess I do get a bit heavy-hearted at times and it shows in my approach to her.*

And that results in her being a bit guarded and reluctant. It becomes a cycle of non-trust and thinking the worst of each other.
OK, so my problems will go away?

Nope. It's a hydra, remember. We are so differently wired that we will never conduct love-making in the same way. Things will improve and change, but you will always be challenged in this regard.
So – I am doomed?

Depends on how you see things. It's a wonderful lifetime challenge, a journey of intimate exploration that only the two of you share. To finish, I would like to ask some advice from you.
Really? Like what?

Wisdom is a funny thing. With age, you begin to understand how much you don't know. Anyway, I think young people have a lot to offer the older generations. My question is: what one thing would you say older couples need that you see missing in their relationships?

Now, that's easy. They need to stay young at heart. Many of the more mature people seem cranky and unfriendly – like they are looking down on the parents of rowdy children.

I see your point. Sara warns me sometimes about turning into a grumpy old man. I can tend to be too serious. When I was young, my older brother used to say to me, 'Lighten up, jerk.' It's kind of become a funny family motto since.

Yes, but there is more to this. Being young in spirit means you are open to learn, keen to give things a go, not afraid to let go, and being up for everything that is on offer.

Go on.

We often quote from the gospel about needing to become like little children but gloss over the preceding part of that verse which says, 'unless you change'.[56] Older people are so often afraid of change, of new things and of anything different. God requires us to be open to change and that is what it means to be young at heart – being up for anything and everything that is of God.

Excellent advice, I shall treasure it. It's been great having this chat.

OK, see you in nearly forty years' time.

Chapter Thirty-One
Tourist to Self

World Events

- During this decade technology exploded – for the first time we had the World Wide Web, web browsers, search engines, Amazon, Google, Netflix, handheld devices, text messages, digital mobile phones, PlayStations, 3-D games, affordable laptops and USB sticks
- Also during this decade our family exploded and grew

I have just survived a 7.8 magnitude earthquake and my face hurts. Why? Well, it's because I can't stop smiling.

The earthquake closed eighty buildings in downtown Wellington where I work so I was forced to remain at home. And this meant more time with two of my grandsons and more fun for me. More fun, more smiles – now my face hurts from being so happy.

Just as I relish being a hands-on grandad so it was back in the 1980s and nineties when my own children were young. I thoroughly basked in being a dad. Simon, Nat and Abi were great kids, and Sara and I found that we loved being parents. Those years flew past us with barely a wave goodbye.

The time with babies is agonisingly short, like a hiccup in the continuum of life. One moment they are helpless and cute, the next they are bouncing all over you and demanding your undivided attention. Preschool is just a moment longer, stacked to the gunwales with learning and change. At least school days linger for a while. Life felt like it had its foot firmly stuck on the accelerator.

Our weekends were busy with family night Fridays, Saturday sports and Sunday church. Finding 'us time' was tricky, but we were blessed with grandparents living across the road once Abi was born.

Nowadays we have several photographs of the kids at various ages and stages. I often pause to relive the memories like trying to recreate the aftertaste of some wonderful meal. I smile at first but if I pause just a moment too long, I get really sad. It becomes like looking at people who are no longer on this earth, and I find myself wondering where these little people have gone to. I seriously ache to have my time with them all over again.

In their place now are big people with families and loved ones of their own. But how can that be? Just a moment ago I was the young dad and they were my little treasures. I can still clearly see their expectant faces when I walked in the door after work and heard the cries of 'Play with me, Daddy'. This would be followed by compulsory rounds of examining the intricacies of the latest Lego invention, or admiring the day's artwork that was always so good it had to be posted on the laundry Wall of Fame.

Now they are off on their own adventures and I am the grandad. My children are like shadows attached to my soul. They will always be with me and go where I go, even if I can no longer touch them.

Consequently, when the opportunity after the earthquake came to spend quality time with the new generation of bright-eyed wonders, I snatched it up. I immediately put on my grandad jeans, the ones that already have holes in the knees from playing on the carpet, and we played for days without having to think too much about the rest of life and its propensity to rush by.

One lesson Sara has been teaching me lately is to be a tourist in my own life. With fresh eyes and a sense of awe, tourists see marvellous things that we residents take for granted. New Zealand is known as Godzone; it is a very beautiful and spectacular country and our clean, green country is heaving with a multitude of tourists. I often walk down the same old roads, past the same sights and chuckle at the buzzy groups from cruise ships excitedly chatting and photographing what I see every day.

Being a tourist in your own life is about appreciating how wonderful life really is. It's about taking time to inhale all the beauty and wonder around you until soaking up the goodness becomes the only oxygen you want to breathe.

Like many, I'm a driven man who lives to achieve – my days are a rush, full of thoughts about what needs to be done. Many people would ache to have a life as blessed as mine, and yet I often find it joyless and flat, especially when I obsess about the next thing instead of savouring the now.

Enjoying the moment like a tourist sustains and enriches us at a whole new level and allows us to smile even when we experience earthquakes that could bring our life to a sudden standstill.

If I could bottle and sell my wife's clever little secret of being a tourist in my own life, I could rival Bill Gates' fortune. But there I go again, gulping down what is ahead of me instead of enjoying each sip.

Message to men (MTM)

Just like in the book of Ecclesiastes, our entire lives seem to be driven by the search for the real meaning of happiness. And yet we only need look around us to find it.

James Oppenheim once said, 'The foolish person seeks happiness in the distance, the wise grows it under his feet.'[57]

Start by looking at the carefree lives of children. It is said that children laugh considerably more often than adults. They also cry more as they seem to be more fully alive. Most children are consumed by what's in front of them, but is that such a bad thing?

One of the greatest blessings you will ever have here on earth right now is your marriage. Don't belittle its potential, or dismiss its wonderful ability to bring you joy and satisfaction.

Ask God for fresh eyes to fully appreciate your wife and all the good she brings into your life. Now, that's a source of real happiness just begging not to be squandered. Don't be one of the sad blokes who realise too late in life what they had all along.

Enjoy the wife you married as a young man! Lovely as an angel,
beautiful as a rose ... never take her love for granted!
Proverbs 5:18b-19, *The Message*

Chapter Thirty-Two
Scary Moments

World Events

- Rwandan genocide kills over 800,000 Tutsis
- Netscape Navigator released and becomes market leader for browsing the web
- A comet hit Jupiter and creates 3,200 kilometre-high fireballs and leaves black bruises in the clouds
- Simon is left behind and becomes lost

Life is full of mix-ups. The confusion which then abounds can be side-splittingly funny or just plain annoying. But worst of all is when it results in scary moments, and there are none so scary as those that involve your own children.

Soon after Abi was born, we began a family tradition in 1994 of travelling to Auckland over the New Year to visit our good friends Nicholas and Michelle. The long eight-hour trip from Wellington necessitated a stopover for the sake of travel-weary children.

Half way through the journey we often called in to see our university mates, Peter and Janelle. He was a doctor and she was a teacher. As dedicated Christians wanting to make a difference in the world, they had decided to live among the poor in a rural spot located in the middle of the North Island.

But it's not so easy to relate to the poor, especially when your status is highly elevated as the only doctor for miles around. This brought about some interesting challenges for Dr Peter.

On our first visit, they were living in a small place with their four children and a bunch of livestock. Peter was horrified when we pulled up in a new car and insisted we park it in his garage out of sight of the locals.

Sara and I had never owned a new car before, and at the time I thought he was just trying to ensure it was kept safe; the township was known for its high crime rate. Unbeknown to me the garage also housed a brood of chickens. The next morning it was my turn to be unimpressed when I found our shiny new Fiat with scratches on the bonnet, covered in chicken poo.

The long and deep discussion we'd had about the poor the night before suddenly seemed meaningless as I drove off the next day leaving behind a fume of annoyance.

When we next visited, they had bought a disused nurses' training home which gave them seventeen bedrooms. Peter always had plans and schemes and this one was to rent to skiers on a room by room basis, which he did for some years.

The place was so long that a scooter was the best way to travel from one end to the other. At that time, they also had a huge St Bernard dog which was very protective of their young ones. Our children weren't so keen on the enormous beast, but it insisted on following them around and keeping a watchful eye on them.

During our first mealtime, we all sat down at the table for dinner when the huge dog brushed past, checking on the new kids. Its tail swept almost everything off the table, sending children scrambling for safety and the adults diving to rescue what they could of the food. Later we thought it funny, but at the time I made up my mind never to own a dog that was bigger than me, or which could create such devastation with just one swish of its wayward tail.

Our long trips were interrupted with bouts of kids being car sick, accusing one another of being in each other's space and, of course, the obligatory, endless 'Are we there yet?' We soon discovered that Nicholas and Michelle lived almost an hour north of Auckland which meant a further trek through New Zealand's busiest city and more of the same from the kids before the adults could enjoy a cool beer together on the deck of their wonderful home near the beach.

One time when Simon was seven years old, we allowed him to accompany Zoe at nine and Jeremy also seven to the nearby estuary. We were told the others did this trip by themselves often. What the adults didn't anticipate was the royal battle that then ensued between the siblings, and like all wars, it is the innocent who suffer the most. Simon was abandoned at the water's edge while the furious Zoe and Jeremy marched their armies of one off in different directions.

Eventually, they both returned home, without Simon. He was lost. While I was happy for him to be beside the water in the company of the others, I was freaking out that he was now there by himself. All sorts of wild scenarios stampeded through my mind.

Search parties were hurriedly arranged and we followed the others back to the estuary only to find that Simon was not there. Now the stampede of horrible thoughts turned into a doomsday image. I have seldom been so scared and angry and all of a flutter. We split into groups and powered around the area frantically looking for one little lost boy.

Time was frozen, but not my fears as I struggled to hold it together, desperate to find my son. After what seemed like a hellish eternity, he was found – having gone to a neighbouring house and announcing clearly and calmly that he was lost, giving full and accurate details of his name, rank and serial number.

This was not the first time he had been lost. Whereas this time it seemed like I was living a nightmare, the previous time had been very funny. Sara and Lesley had taken toddler Simon to the exciting new mall at Coastlands on the Kapiti Coast out of Wellington. Engrossed in shopping, the responsible adults had left Simon playing by himself and gone to different stores both thinking the other was looking after our three-year-old.

When they met up, there was no Simon. But before they could push the panic button, an announcement was made across the complex for the parents of Simon Michael Carey to please come to the information booth. Those hours of training little Simon to repeat his name and where he lived had paid off.

That night I got home to a very sheepish wife and a boisterous toddler who couldn't wait to tell his daddy that he had lost Mummy but that she was found. My heart skipped a beat until I saw the funny side of it all.

This same lad was to unintentionally do a similar thing to my poor heart many years later. We were at a church camp with visiting speakers from South Africa. During the free time, I was playing tennis, trying to exact revenge on mates who had beaten me earlier. The rest of the camp were lazing about, or playing soccer in a nearby field.

Just as we were finishing, the triumphant smile was wiped off my face when someone ran to the court to say that Simon had collapsed on the pitch and they were administering CPR to him. I sprinted faster than was possible for my lumbering frame, wondering what I would find.

My heart was pounding in my chest. I was exhausted after my hard-won tennis match, the summer heat and the incredible anxiety that one of my beloved children may have just died. When I got there, I could see everyone standing around, but no sign of my lad.

Then I found Simon lying on the ground with our good friends Julian and Claire calmly working to revive him. But it wasn't my Simon, it was the visiting speaker of the same name. In the panic that followed, people had passed on the messages that Simon had collapsed and a well-meaning person had misinformed me. My teenage boy was off calling for the ambulance.

I just dropped on the spot and sobbed with relief. Then I sobbed some more with combined grief and guilt that someone else's son was lying there. The emotions were overwhelming and I found it hard to breathe for a while.

Eventually the ambulance came and the paramedics took over while we all sat around the field praying. By now my Simon had returned and I hugged him long and hard and sobbed some more.

Simon Petit died that day – you could say in place of my son Simon. He was a wonderful man of God with a great sense of humour who preached powerful messages that rocked your soul. That day was truly one of the scariest in my life. But God never wastes a calamity or catastrophe. All the time that this was going on, one of the lads' mothers was watching how the Christians responded. The authenticity of the people at the camp somehow allowed the love of God to shine through with genuine hope that Simon was in a better place. He was with the Lord he had always loved so much, calling on his name even with his dying breath.

This lovely lady had had such a hard life but as my pastor, Pete, recently said, 'Life is a journey and it's never too late to change course.' On that day, she became a Christian and so began her own kingdom journey towards a life of faith.

Mix-ups happen. We never know what life is going to throw at us. When I was a teenager I worked for a cannery. Tins of food were sold to staff a dozen at a time for ten cents each. Some were dented and usually they had no labels. Coming from a poor background I made full use of this perk, bringing home enough to make a stack that went floor to ceiling in our laundry.

We had great fun as a family trying to guess the contents of each can. Often, we would open one for pudding that contained pet food instead of peaches, or tomatoes instead of baked beans for dinner.

Life can be like that – unpredictable, confusing, mixed up, but there is often a funny side and beyond doubt, God is always at work. These cans are like our lives, a mystery to us. The only label they need is a warning that says: 'Contains traces of God.'

Message to men (MTM)

Jesus said in 1 John 4:18, 'There is no fear in love.' We are not meant to live lives of dread and anxiety. As Christians, we know the end of the story, so what are we so scared of?

In Matthew 10:28, Jesus also warned us not to be afraid of those who would harm our bodies but cannot destroy our souls. He was saying, 'Come on guys, get an eternal perspective here. See the big picture and stop shaking with fear like some frightened child.'

As men, the cliché still holds that we need to grow some and not be ruled by fear and worry. Being positive about life and optimistic around trouble is very contagious. Our family look to us at such times. We need courage and grit to be a calm head in stressful times as that brings clear thinking whereas panic just distorts everything.

I admire my wife's positive outlook on life and her sayings like, 'It's just a bump on the road of life.' She is a living lesson to me of not being fearful.

Albert Einstein once allegedly said, 'Stay away from negative people. They have a problem for every solution.'

Anxiety weighs down the heart ...
Proverbs 12:25

Thirty-Three
The Sting and the Storms

World Events

- The Spice Girls rocket to fame
- Dolly arrives, the world's first cloned sheep
- Prince Charles and Princess Diana divorce
- I travel a lot with Foreign Affairs and Trade

This week I was swarmed by angry wasps. This is not a pleasant experience, as I found out when I foolishly disturbed a nest in my garden. Despite running faster than the speed of light I still suffered a dozen or so stings. It felt like I had been repeatedly beaten with a crowbar. But the real problem was what came next.

I was already hot after an hour's work, but began sweating profusely after the mad dash to safety. Fear and anxiety added to the torture as I had no idea whether I might experience a severe reaction to so many stings. What made things worse was that I was home alone and I knew I had only a few minutes to determine whether I was allergic or not before I needed to get help.

Self-examination does not really help at times like this as everything is exaggerated and larger than life. I could have sworn that my chest felt tight, or was that just the poison of anxiety creeping through my body? Staying calm is essential, so I reassured myself and lay on the couch with several ice packs while I waited for Sara Nightingale to swoop through the door with life-saving antihistamine.

Two handbags purchased and forty minutes later, Sara and Lesley found me still sweating, in pain, but most of all needing reassurance, like all men during a self-made crisis.

Stuff happens. Life is a roller coaster of events, sometimes taking you on a ride you would rather not be on. Like the wasp stings, what matters is how you react to what comes your way.

The stings hurt, but anaphylactic reactions can cause death. Bee and wasp stings account for more deaths in the US than from any creature other than humans. In Australia deaths from bee and wasp stings are on a par with snake bites. Only the mosquito kills more humans worldwide.[58]

Looking back to the 1990s, there were several events that were painful, but in the end, it was our reaction to them that mattered the most. It still amazes me how two people can go through the same painful event where one learns from it and blossoms while the other turns inward, clutching onto bitterness and anger. Thank God for my wonderfully positive wife, who always led the way in finding the good in every circumstance. It is something I have had to grow into.

Leonard Ravenhill tells a story of tourists visiting a picturesque village. In a rather patronising way, one of the visitors asked an old man sitting by a fence, 'Were any great men born in this village?' Without looking up the old man replied, 'No, only babies.'[59]

Great people are made by how they react to what life brings their way. In a similar fashion, great marriages are carved out of our reactions to life and especially to each other.

Three young children can only mean busyness, drama and full-on days without much respite. Drifting apart in your marriage can happen unnoticed as the focus is almost entirely on the little ones running between your legs and climbing up your back wanting and needing endless attention.

I changed jobs soon after Abi was born and went from pioneering technology at the Fire Service to being a director at Foreign Affairs and Trade (a government department). This meant overseas travel, lots of out-of-hours events and giving speeches at conferences, all the while trying to be the best dad and husband I could be.

My reaction to these new demands was carefully and deliberately geared so that our marriage would not suffer, nor would I become an absent father. For example, I insisted that Sara be invited to attend most of the social functions with me. At times, the organisers would refuse, but the more forward-thinking ones realised the benefit of having partners along and would extend the invitation accordingly.

During my trips abroad, I would save my daily allowance by living off homemade muesli I'd smuggled into the country and going to the nearest McDonald's in the evenings. The extra cash would then be spent on presents for my family. I often came home with a suitcase bulging with goodies.

The kids loved it and the tradition became that we would sit around the mat in the lounge while I dived into the case, dishing out present after present. I hadn't learned the benefits of quality in those days so the toys were often poorly made and would break within a few days, as I have mentioned before in this book. But I didn't care and nor did the kids, knowing full well that another Daddy Santa visit would come along soon enough.

Rightly so Sara would scold me, telling me to buy just one special present for each family member. But I couldn't help myself as I often visited several countries and would use my spare time wandering the shops thinking about what to get them.

I suppose it's a reaction to those days of being poor as a child. Rather than learning to better appreciate what is in front of me, I have a tendency to want more. More is not always best. Being in the now and enjoying what you have is superior by far.

In 1990 Sara bought me an atlas as a present and wrote inside it: 'Travel in here is free!' We had never expected to travel as money was always very tight, but all that changed when I joined Foreign Affairs and Trade. In fact, just before I left the Fire Service I spent two weeks cruising across Canada looking at rural fire-fighting software. A small group of us toured by car, plane and helicopter visiting parts of the country that few Canadians would ever get to see.

Travel was exciting but always involved what is termed the re-entry issue. Coming home after a time of absence I needed to re-establish my place in a family which had been getting along fine without me. It's a shock to realise the family can be happy and do cool things without you being the centre of it all. My reaction to this wasn't always great, but I worked hard not to feel like I was a part-time member of my family.

As the children grew a little older, Pop and Lesley also looked after them for longer times so that Sara could travel with me overseas occasionally. Treats like these were invaluable to replenishing our relationship and renewing our love. They more than compensated for the strain of being parents to our little ones.

However, these trips were not without their own dramas. On one such trip we visited Russia. I had been warned that as soon as they saw my diplomatic passport the Russians would take away my bags for closer inspection. Foolishly, we didn't have spare clothes in our cabin bags and both our bags 'went missing' for several days. We were stranded in a foreign country – Sara in high heels and a short skirt and me with formal meetings to attend without a change of clothes.

The diplomatic car picked us up from the hotel the next day. Sadly, I had to abandon a very unhappy wife at the gates of the embassy while I attended business meetings. But as Winston Churchill supposedly said, 'Attitude is a little thing that makes a big difference.'[60] So, after a few tears, Sara checked her reaction to the bad situation and decided to make the most of it. Without even the comforts of appropriate clothing she hobbled around the cobblestones of Red Square taking in as many of the sights as she could. Despite acquiring a few blisters, she arrived back at the embassy at midday beaming about her day thus far. At that point, the attaché took us out to the 'best restaurant in town'. After a twenty-minute walk, we arrived at an American burger bar. By now Sara's feet were bleeding and she was visibly gutted that we were not eating authentic local cuisine. As a foodie, this was supposed to be the highlight of her visit. But again, she tempered her reaction and made the most of it.

At this point I would say that she was a true star, but there was more to come. On returning to the embassy, the ambassador's wife appeared and invited Sara to see the sights with her.

Delighted, Sara took her up on the offer, only to discover that the ambassador's wife's car was in the garage and that they would have to walk and go by tube everywhere. I don't know how she did it, but when she arrived back later in the day, she was full of smiles and chit-chat. However, when the attaché offered us a ride back to the hotel I think she was the first one to leap into the car.

That evening she ordered room service and tucked herself away in a deep bubble bath for hours, soaking away the aches and pains. The day was a challenge from go to whoa but it was my incredible wife's reaction to each event that made the real difference. I would not say she was a star – she was more like a galaxy!

Wasps sting and so does life at times. It's our reaction to these that matters most. Positive reactions are good choices, and a life full of good choices is a life worth living. A marriage full of the same is the best there is.

Message to men (MTM)

Charles Spurgeon once said, 'It was with great perseverance the snail reached the ark.'[61]

Perseverance is a quality we all admire. We relish movies where the hero is knocked down time and time again, but somehow, they dig deep to find the strength to rise once more and conquer evil. We love it! But perseverance comes with a price. It takes many trials and hardships to build this into our character. And with each blow we suffer hurt.

Marriage is multidimensional in this regard. On one hand, it builds lasting resilience by tapping into deep strength that comes from being two, not one. But it also comes with many challenges that require great loyalty and determination to master.

This book has touched on some of the many things I have put my long-suffering wife through. Despite this, she is utterly dedicated to me.

She is an anchor to me when I drift and a pillar when I buckle under life's burdens.

I may be nothing more than a snail in this great universe, but with a love like that when combined with the love of God I will make the ark one day.

Many claim to have unfailing love,
but a faithful person who can find?
Proverbs 120:6

Chapter Thirty-Four
Fat Bottoms

World Events
- The first *Harry Potter* book released
- Mike Tyson bites off part of Evander Holyfield's ear
- In NZ, the median age is a sprightly thirty-three. Two decades later it has increased to thirty-seven
- As a family we love biking everywhere

Mark Twain had a way with words that uncannily seems to sum up my life. He once quipped, 'Get a bicycle. You will not regret it if you live.'[62]

It's true that a bicycle once cost me dearly when I had a serious encounter with a loose seat that put me in hospital with torsion of the testicle. Until proven otherwise, we were not at all sure that it hadn't also cost us the possibility of having a family. But riding is in my veins, so it's no surprise that it also runs in the blood of all the Careys. We serious riders have strong chiselled calves and tight bottoms from hours of pumping our legs. And my wife loves it – the legs, that is.

Sara and I had started our married life riding ten-speed pushbikes. The first time we took our shiny new mobiles for a ride it turned out rather a longer trip than anticipated. I adored feeling the wind on my face and pushing myself hard, so I rode on with enthusiasm. Charles M. Schultz, creator of the Peanuts comic strip, once said: 'Life is like a ten speed bicycle. Most of us have gears we never use.'[63] Well, on this day I was using every available gear and putting my heart and soul into the ride.

I was so enraptured with the experience that I forgot about my new bride, until I realised that she was no longer alongside me. Warily pivoting in the saddle (to ensure it wasn't loose) I saw her in the distance, stopped by the side of the road. Showing off my riding skills I rocketed back in no time to find her in a flood of tears. She was finding biking much harder than expected and was convinced she could never come to love such torture. Happily, this proved not to be so. As our fitness improved and our bottoms tightened, we rode our bikes across Dunedin and beyond for over two years. Without the aid of modern Lycra, gel seats or padded shorts, some of our rides were extremely challenging to our nether regions.

Through our riding, we accidentally came upon one of life's best-kept secrets – that is: *those that play together, stay together*. A good marriage involves fostering common interests, building on lots of experiences which deeply bond our souls together, even when it hurts.

Too many couples find that when they retire, they don't have much in common. They are like strangers to each other, invading each other's territory; being together is not something to be cherished, but dreaded. During the fast-paced years of life, they failed to have fun together and become the best of friends.

Over the decades, I have learned to garden. Sara was born a natural gardener, it is a creative expression of who she is. At one time, I was guilty of treating everything remotely green as if it needed to be mowed, painted, or weeded. But over the years gardening has become something we do together; we love getting stuck in and working alongside each other. It's real Team Carey therapeutic fun.

On the other hand, Sara has learned to enjoy skiing. Despite many false starts and a few incidents we would rather forget, a day skiing together under crispy blue skies on lovely powder snow is as good as it gets. Fishing is something we have both enjoyed from the get-go, although I must confess to secret envy when she constantly out-fishes me.

Back to biking – this soon became a family event. When the children were young, we bought dazzling two-wheelers with child seats. What great adventures we had whizzing around town, often with a child slumped on the back fast asleep. We especially liked riding to church. At first this was much to the chagrin of friends who had just spent fifteen minutes getting their uncooperative families strapped into cars for a five-minute drive, and then wrestling for another ten minutes getting them out. Before long the joy of biking spread and the church exterior was dotted with bicycles of all shapes and sizes.

Of course, as the kids grew older they got their own bikes and spent many happy hours riding up and down our shared driveway, building ramps and obstacles to play on. As the designated handyman, I would spend ages on maintenance for some wayward tricycle, and adjusting the bicycles as the kids grew.

Middle childhood was a great time to get into mountain bike riding. This became a regular after-church activity for me and the boys. One time, we rode the Rimutaka Incline, a disused railway line that has a tunnel at the end which is nearly a kilometre long. None of our torches were powerful enough to penetrate the utter darkness.

Even as an adult I have to say it was really scary. Nobody wanted to be first as they just couldn't see, and nobody wanted to be last, in case – who knows what. But we did it – only to realise we had to ride all the way back again.

As you can imagine, when we got home, the boys ran inside to tell their mum of the scariest ride in the world. I, however, leapt in the car and bought the biggest Maglite® I could find. The next time we did the Incline, armed with the light of lights, the whole tunnel was lit up.

Sara's brother, Buncle, was the main protagonist with mountain biking. He was always a fantastic rider who wowed everyone with his speed and skill. In our eyes, Buncle could do anything, but he had a particular knack of being able to motor up the steepest hills imaginable without stopping or falling off. Like all wonderful uncles, he liked to show off to his nephews and niece and so he would challenge us to ride up a particular hill that only he had conquered. Most of us would struggle only a few metres before we tumbled in a heap.

Years later, when they were in their early twenties, he made the same challenge to the boys and their good friend Martin. My sons made a good fist of it but inevitably failed. Then to everyone's surprise, Martin climbed on his bike and rode to the top without faltering. Unfortunately, Buncle had been overconfident and offered $100 to anyone who could conquer the slope. The eager lads made sure their uncle paid up.

At times, we would have twenty or more children and adults turn up for our rides through the parks and reserves surrounding Lower Hutt. We would go riding no matter the weather, through muddy rivers, along steep banks and down tracks until we were all happily exhausted. It's a magical feeling at the end of a ride when you are covered in dirt and grime but have a grin so wide it lasts well into the week. Everyone looked forward to our outings.

Simon and I did a few more serious road trips, biking into Wellington and back one day. It took us many hours but we felt like heroes. Riding along a motorway is scary stuff, especially when huge articulated trucks fly past, sucking all the wind in their direction. But my most famous road trip (one that became a family legend, at least in my mind) was from home in Lower Hutt, up the coast to Pop and Lesley's holiday house. It was around sixty kilometres along the main state highway. In hindsight, the distance wasn't much, but to me and in the eyes of my family, I was a superdad who could do amazing feats of daring. Little did they know I had had to stop several times, not due to tiredness, but because of my aching backside. The achievement was regarded by all as 'magnificent' and so every time we drove the steep hills, I would annoyingly ask the family whether they knew that I had ridden over it on my bike. Inevitably their eyes would roll and the tuts would come, but I secretly knew their admiration remained through the years.

Soon after that I felt brave enough to begin biking to work on a regular basis, a round trip of about two hours. Until then, I was carpooling with four bulky guys crammed into a tiny Mini with our sports bags and sandwiches. To be sure it was economical, but not very comfortable as the poor wee car struggled under its enormous burden. However, on the day we had a puncture and couldn't get the jack to work we found that three guys could easily lift a Mini while the fourth removed the wheel. Alas all good things must come to an end. The traffic steadily got worse over the years and our driver wanted to go earlier and earlier, which would have meant I would miss my daily devotional readings with Simon. So, I started riding.

Riding to work soon become my modus operandi. My fitness climbed to an all-time high, especially when combined with the gym. I became very enthusiastic and started convincing others to ride to work as well. Biking was cheap, great for the health and largely independent of traffic jams. It was an excellent way to mentally wind down at the end of the day and feel good about yourself, especially when weaving in and out of traffic that was stopped for as far as the eye could see.

These days I still bike as often as I can, but usually in the safety of the gym. I plug in some decent worship music and ride my heart out for most of the session. I have caught myself once or twice singing out loud but I don't care.

My local grandsons at age five and three also love going for rides on the back of the bicycles with Mum, Dad and the grandies. When he was just one, little Asher (Nat's son) would try to climb on the bike in the garage as his way of telling us he wanted to go out for a buzzy bike ride in the fresh air.

I find riding with my grandchildren and hammering the exercise bike at the gym very relaxing. Chris Hallman is alleged to have said: 'Life may not be about your bike, but it sure can help you get through it.'[64] It is hard to be sad when you are riding a bike, even when you are going nowhere except on a journey to fitness and avoiding the onset of fat bottoms.

Message to men (MTM)

Here's a really touchy subject – keeping yourself and your marriage in shape.

Statistically, once men marry they put on the beef, over 2.5kg annually in the first five years. It appears the pressure is off; we no longer need to win the hand of our beloved. Quite rapidly it seems we blokes develop that contented rounded middle. I know, as I have one. It is small but it still annoys me.

Added to this downward spiral, we can relapse into sloppy clothing and habits. This is a major turn-off for our more fashion-conscious partners. But probably worst of all is that we forget to 'date' our wives, to do special things with them and for them. What seems so natural when we were courting now becomes a chore.

What can we do about it? Eating is a joint activity where we influence each other for better or worse. So, agree on smaller portions, save puddings for special occasions, train your stomachs to cope with less and better food.

Add to this by going to the gym together or playing sport as a couple. For us, walks and talks are the best. Whatever you choose – do something three times a week, and do it together. Yes, you will ooze sweat, but your glow signals to her that she is worth it and that you still highly value what she thinks of you.

Pause before you dress. Ask your wife her opinions on your clothes. Make her your fashion adviser. And now the hardest but most rewarding of all. Take her on marriage dates. Plan these, protect these and then ensure they are loads of fun.

By making a sustained effort you are shaping things that matter the right way. Both your marriage and your life will enjoy greater longevity for it.

Lazy people want much but get little, but those who work hard will prosper.
Proverbs 13:4, NLT

Chapter Thirty-Five
The Gang

World Events

- The population of earth's wild mammals, birds, amphibians, fish and other vertebrates declined by more than half in forty years
- Using today's food prices, Sara and I would have spent around $600,000 on groceries over forty years
- The gang of eight we are part of have been friends for more than 350,000 hours

The very first thing Sara ever sent me was a card that said: 'Don't walk in front of me… I may not follow. Don't walk behind me… I may not lead. Walk beside me… just be my friend.'[65]

I was mystified by this. Was she telling me that I was too bossy, or worse, hinting that I was a wimp? For days, I replayed past events in my mind which could have been interpreted either way. It drove me crazy.

Then it dawned on me that all she was saying was that good relationships are founded on friendship. And that is exactly what we have based our marriage on for the last thirty-nine years. Yes, we are husband and wife, but even better than that we are best friends, soulmates, confidantes who choose above all else to be in each other's company and to do things together.

But friendship doesn't need a contract or a licence and it isn't symbolised by a ring on the finger – it is represented by an unspoken connection to another person, no matter what. It has enduring qualities that are weatherproof and impervious to time, that seem to magnify the best in you and minimise your faults.

Around such companions, you are completely safe to be yourself. In fact, as Erwin T. Randall mentioned, real friends don't see you as a fool even when you are occasionally foolish.[66] Although friendship is the very glue by which we have built our marriage, it is bigger than who we are, extending beyond Team Carey. We have a bunch of mates we call the Gang of Eight which started as a group of four college girls when Sara was just thirteen. This was an era in which a move of God swept the country resulting in many of Sara's friends becoming committed Christians. These school chums stayed close throughout their teens, eventually marrying Christian blokes who also became lifelong buddies, thus forming the Gang of Eight.

Four became eight and then the children made a clan of nineteen. That's mind-numbing enough, but there was more to come – the Gang now has quite a dynasty. Over a period of forty-four years, the four transmogrified into forty-two once grandchildren started popping up to say hello.

Most of the Gang I have known for four decades and my life is full of wonderful memories of their special friendship, even though in the early days our paths diverged a lot.

One duo had children straight away and kept producing them almost before the others had started. In those days, theirs was a hectic life with four young boys running them ragged, little money and a very busy time either farming, or at Bible college, or owning a garage.

Ours was a gentler approach to family. Despite marrying young, we waited almost seven years before careening down the fast slopes of parenting three spritely monsters.

One of the other pairs married later and took a steady path to building their careers while balancing the arrival of two children.

The last twosome to marry were our high-flyers who charged at life with seemingly endless pockets of money and energy. They were the last to begin their family.

When the second generation were young, visits to other Gang Headquarters were rare but always welcomed. The entire Gang has never lived in the same city, but over time the kids grew to know each other as we began to have more frequent get-togethers.

Ivan and Lydia (part of the gang) would come to our house, where the girls would snuggle down for a weekend of mystifying girly things while the lads took on the great outdoors. Us boys would drive over to the Coast Road through Wainuiomata and, having hunted and captured our fish and chips, we would then set off to find a good camping spot in the forest park.

These events never ever went without a hitch. On the very first night, Nat was violently sick. It proved to be a battle for rest, let alone sleep, tending to Nat and trying to block out Ivan's snoring. And yet we went back multiple times. During the next visit to the forest, the boys kept calling out, 'Dad! We can see the stars.'

It was a windy night, marginal for tenting, so I thought the flap had blown open. I finally climbed out of my tent to find theirs had ripped down the middle, leaving them lying under the night sky in their sleeping bags. But no matter what happened we always returned home triumphant, full of manly tales at having conquered the wild.

Time passed and we decided to brave all nineteen of the mob camping together. We chose El Rancho where Sara and I had met and where most of the Gang had been leaders at one time or another. It was not just a place of great sentimental value, but also far more civilised than a forest park.

Of course, the offspring wanted grander adventures than just sleeping in a canvas city, so they built their own bivouac in a nearby woodland. Lucky for us adults, one of the older boys, a teenager, agreed to supervise during the night.

Somehow, I got the job as the designated grown-up. One by one I was called to bring the kids back to our tent sites. Starting from the youngest to oldest, once they heard the night noises of nocturnal animals and the creaking of trees, they abandoned their makeshift home of twigs and leaves. In the end, the only person left was the teenager, who had slept through it all. He was surprised when he woke in the morning to find that he was home alone in his bivvy.

These times and other trips to El Rancho cemented the friendships of our children. Many of them have stayed steadfast buddies with several flatting together and generally doing life with one another. They have attended each other's weddings and been travelling companions during overseas trips.

The affection we have for each other is very real. I have had the fun of working with Sebastian (another member of the gang) in several capacities; the first time when we were both contractors for a telecommunications company that was in disarray. Sebastian has a wicked sense of humour and began teasing me about my daily banana ration. A competition soon formed over the most original way to use the stickers that come plastered on each banana. Creativity blossomed. Once, I arrived in the morning to find my mouse wouldn't work. Being a quasi-geek, I tested the cords, rebooted the computer and even checked to see that the drivers were installed. It wasn't until I turned the mouse over that I discovered a banana sticker blotting out the optical sensor.

Technically I was Sebastian's boss so 'revenge was mine'. The next day, Sebastian unknowingly wandered around the building with a banana sticker on his backside having sat on one that I had strategically placed on his chair. Putting it there was no easy task as by then we were highly suspicious of being caught out. This manoeuvre required a distraction worthy of a magician, just before he sat down.

The banana games reached Olympic heights as we continued competing for months. But eventually I was awarded the gold medal in the form of a banana-shaped box to keep my prize safe. The banana protector looked a little rude and left me a bit embarrassed when pulling it out of my lunch bag. Inevitably, some passer-by would stop to ask what it was, always leaving with a wry smile or a suppressed giggle. In hindsight, maybe Sebastian was real victor in the banana kingdom. I may have to wait many years, but I plan to have the last laugh. Sebastian is also eight years younger than the rest of us and therefore, the elected caregiver for when we are old and doddery.

Nowadays, the Gangsters like to gather numerous times a year. We have made it a tradition to spend Easter together, usually at our cottage by the mountain. It is always a food-fest, with Ivan being a chef and most of the others serious foodies. Sebastian supplies the cellared wine and often we use wild ingredients from scrumping, which Natalie (Sebastian's wife) and I like to do (much to the mortification of the others).

This tradition has been hard to keep with one of the couples, Dennis and Diana, living in Australia for some time. So, one year we invaded the land of Oz, forcing Australians to part with large quantities of delicious wine and absorbing all their beautiful sunshine for ourselves while driving around the countryside by car and motorbike.

The next generation are always keen to muscle in on these events as they know the quality of the meals and the fun times we have. But it is tricky, especially with so many little ones. Today, decades after the Gang started, we are scattered across five countries.

All of us have had our share of defining moments. This friendship which we so fondly call the Gang of Eight has been an amazing source of strength and joy. A few years back when times were very hard for Sara and me, it was the Gang who played a significant role in breaking through the mist and the mire. When the storms of anxiety, depression and stress raged against us, their friendship gave us shelter. They brought to us liberating words from God and provided listening ears when many others spoke only platitudes and imposed solutions. When adversity came, they were there waiting in the wings to fight on our behalf by praying for us. As Aristotle said long ago, 'The antidote for fifty enemies is one friend.'[67]

Others too have had to ride the waves of change, some of it unwanted and unpredictable.

We have sat beside the hospital bed of our oldest patched[68] member wondering if he would die after he was hit while riding his bike. That same couple has surprised us as we watched them morph from their cautious disposition to pioneering spirits, moving from the capital city to build a 'bed and breakfast' on a rural property.

We have witnessed another's entrepreneurial ideas and numerous start-up businesses take him and his wife from riches to rags and hopefully back again. Selling a business in the early days netted a fine haul of cash and like all of the Gang, they were generous to a fault, spending a good portion of it on others less fortunate than themselves. The rest of the money was invested into business ventures over the years that have proved to be Teflon™ in nature.

We have watched that 'first married couple' change from young parents struggling to make ends meet to being professionals with qualifications, skills and experience that has secured them work in Australia, England and Canada. At one stage, the husband took literally the quote, 'When life gets complicated I ride.'[69] He left his job and rode his Triumph motorbike for many months around the endless coast of Australia following a passion to explore remote lighthouses.

Several members are petrol-heads indulging in sports cars, expensive SUVs and even a ride-on mower. This seems to be driven by some strange desire to live on adrenaline, which me and my run-of-the-mill Toyota will never understand. But what I can grasp is the magpie instinct to collect things. I have acquired 1,500 DVDs over the years, while others have amassed expensive wines, shoes, businesses and even travel destinations.

Like most kiwis, we like to travel when the budget allows, and even when it doesn't. Between us we have clocked up dozens of countries and had our share of adventures and mishaps. Often these trips are justified in our minds by visiting children, or taking them with us on biking tours or sailing trips.

Life has surrendered much to the Gang and we have seen a lot. But what none of us saw coming was age creeping up on us. Our minds say we are still teenagers, but our bodies tell a different story. By stealth, our head colours seemed to have faded to grey, white or salty brown and even pink. Baldness rules in the majority of the blokes, and all eight of us suffer from hair growing in unwanted places.

Menopause has also assaulted our lovely wives, some getting over it almost before it began while others have been cruelly harassed for ten years or more. Even in the depths of winter it is not uncommon to have to open a window or door to cool down one or more of our hot ladies.

We are eight different personalities from diverse backgrounds. Some of us are a little crazy, some a bit conservative – some are very adventurous while others are very careful. Life has provided us with our fair portion of imperfections and peculiarities.

It seems it was the pious Oliver Cromwell in the seventeenth century who famously said something like, 'Paint me as I am, warts and all.' Good friendships and true friends overlook the foibles and follies. Our best buddies help us see ourselves in positive ways, despite the warts. Rare friends like these laugh with you, cry with you and aren't afraid to be straight with you. That is what makes them so special. This precious friendship is beyond anything that can be bought or forced into being. The Gang of Eight is epitomised by the Sicilian proverb: 'Only your real friends will tell you when your face is dirty.'

The Gang of Eight has endured for so long that it has become part of who I am, adding a richness and depth to my life by 'just being my friends'.

Message to men (MTM)

As men, we love to be the hero in our lives and to those around us. And so, we are quick to adopt a 'lone ranger' persona, someone who rides into bad situations and sorts them out, with all guns blazing.

We often idolise the Mr Fix It, the strong silent type, who can do anything.

This solo act in our lives is not always healthy in a relationship. It's no longer just about you; another person is intimately and intrinsically involved.

God is also at work. Marriages are one of the main building blocks of his Church and he is vitally interested in seeing them become strong.

To become a great husband and not just a good man, you need to let your partner and others in, and give control over to your heavenly Father.

Making yourself vulnerable may seem a weak thing to do but it's not. God has a grand plan for good for both of you.

Kemo sabe, it's time to take the mask off and find out who you can really become with a trusted wife by your side and the God Almighty blazing the way ahead for you.

What a person desires is unfailing love …
Proverbs 19:22

Chapter Thirty-Six
The Big Picture

World Events

- Despite being *Time* magazine's 'Man of the Year', Bill Clinton has an affair with Monica Lewinsky
- Google is founded
- Europeans agree on a single currency – the Euro
- We set in motion moving to the UK

Einstein is known for having said, 'I want to know how God created this world. I am not interested in this or that phenomenon, in the spectrum of this or that element. I want to know his thoughts; the rest are details.'[70]

God, the Master Chef, was cooking up a feast in our lives but, as a young family in the mid to late 1990s, too often all we could see was the baking rather than the baker.

The church we were in at the time was turning itself inside out. Despite all its failings, it had become our home. Its members weren't perfect and a lot of them weren't Christians, but as Eeyore from Winnie-the-Pooh has been attributed as stating, 'Weeds are flowers too, once you get to know them.'[71]

Over the years, we'd had our battles concerning pews, worship music, the raising of hands, buildings and just about anything else that comes to mind. For instance, the church was largely against alcohol – probably a 'hangover' from the Temperance days. One time during the Children's talk our pastor asked what everybody's favourite drink was. Our two-year-old, Abi, stood on the pew and shouted with all her might, 'Alcohol!' There was no use trying to explain to the shocked congregation that friends had just taught her the word as a joke; many of them already knew the dark secret that we brewed our own beer.

Judgement was rife in the church and it was hard not to get caught up in it. Some of the older men would pray mini-sermons that were a thinly veiled rebuke for something they did not approve of. It seemed that nothing was ever good enough. Like the old African proverb goes, 'A goat is never pronounced innocent if the judge is a leopard.'

All that stuff was bad enough, and barely tolerable at times, but the real problem came when the pastor suffered burnout. He had never recovered from the death of his son and the suicide of a close friend whom he was counselling. Eventually he just stopped work and did not return after twelve months of sick leave.

The result was a divided church, some trying in faith to see the big picture while others were sharpening the axe to finish off the wounded. Tensions hit an all-time high.

The situation reminded me of years ago while at Lake Waikaremoana, when I went on a bush-crashing course with the local rangers. The objective was to learn to trust your navigation aids and to work as a team. The group of relatively inexperienced trampers (hikers) were given maps and compasses and taken to a very dense part of the forest. After some preliminary instructions, we were let loose to find our way out without the help of the rangers.

It was not long before people began to argue over which way to go. The sheer number and size of the trees quickly became oppressive, dominating everything in our field of vision. Panic began to rise among the group, and so did mutiny. Half the group were convinced we were going around in circles, wanting to throw away the compass and force their way to a nearby ridge.

Voices were raised, ears were blocked and tears flowed. The other half, including me, still trusted the navigational aids and thought ploughing blindly into a dense forest was foolhardy.

In an angry huff, the group split and went separate ways. Ours eventually found the rendezvous point, with much relief and a little smugness. The ranger shadowing the other group intervened before they got into serious trouble. Afterwards as we sat around the camp and listened to the debriefing, every single person present had miraculously become very teachable.

Church life can be similar to this. We have our map, which is the Word of God. We have our compass, the Holy Spirit, and our guides, the leaders. But there are always the complicators, those who know better, who convince others that the map is out of date or the compass faulty, pointing in the wrong direction. They claim that the guides don't know what they are talking about and so set off in a totally different direction, crashing through and causing damage as they go. These people soon become lost and bitter, blaming everyone else for what has happened to them. I am deeply saddened to say there are many Christians who have strayed in this way. They lose all perspective of the big picture, getting bogged down by the details of life instead of seeking to know God's thoughts.

It was like that back then. The church began falling apart. The finances dried up and we were threatened with bankruptcy.

Together, Sara and I, along with a small bunch of hard-working people, tried to salvage things. Sara took on the role of treasurer and taught Sunday school and we both had oversight of the children's work. We preached, organised other speakers, were small group leaders, and ran the leadership group.

At that stage, Simon was around eleven years old and beginning to show signs of being a restless, bored teenager at church. As there were no activities for the older kids, he had to sit through the sermon.

Everyone seemed preoccupied with their own challenges. I was one of them and so when I said out loud to one of the children's workers that we needed something for teenagers, I was caught short by her reply. She challenged me to consider running something myself. And so I added to my busyness by beginning a group for pre-teens and teenagers called 'Rippling Roots'. We hadn't done this before as we had no teenagers in the church, or so we thought. But once we started the group, kids seemed to come out of the woodwork and before long we had added a dozen more equally disinterested teenagers.

Being a Christian is not boring, it's incredibly interesting, so I grabbed the challenge with both hands. I adopted the approach of Jesus, who made use of everyday objects and activities to get across his spiritual point. At one stage, we performed the gospel message in front of the church using yo-yos while doing a 'Christian' rap. We baked, we used chatter rings[72] and almost anything of topical interest to the teens.

For some time, Simon and I had made a habit of having breakfast together and reading from a booklet called *Topz*.[73] This series was geared to particular age groups, used a cartoon style to get the message across and had activities for the children to do. Simon devoured it. Nat never wanted to join in, but used to have his breakfast conveniently nearby and listen. His was a style of learning by association.

Together we did this for years and now the input began to pay off as Simon became my right-hand person at Rippling Roots. His faith took a mighty leap forward and he was responsible for bringing along several of his friends.

During this time, we did what we could to support our grieving pastor. Unfortunately, he totally withdrew from everyone, making it clear that he wanted no contact while he got better.

It is times like these that people's true natures are revealed and many could not see beyond themselves. I find it amazing how people get stuck in a hall of mirrors, only seeing themselves no matter which way they turn. A faction wanted the pastor gone, being very vocal that he should never had been appointed in the first place. Others couldn't take the pressure and left. The troubling thing for us was that most of our closest friends also left. One couple went to live among the poor in a nearby city, another couple went down to the South Island, partly to support ageing parents. Other sets of good friends had left to live in Auckland and the Bay of Plenty. And so, we found ourselves largely friendless, trying to do everything in the church to keep it afloat. Despite our superhuman efforts, each way we turned we seemed to tread on kryptonite. It would have been so easy to throw away the compass and crash on in a different direction in some mistaken belief that we knew where we were going. But since we had been one of the main supporters in the pastor being appointed, we wanted to do the right thing by him, so we persisted.

Sara and I were exhausted by then and seriously on the brink of burnout ourselves. Part way through the year, I had been to England for a job interview with an organisation that was part of the justice system. Arriving early in the morning at Heathrow Airport, I barely had time to shave and change into a suit in the toilets before I was straight into eight hours of interviews, psychometric testing and workshops.

Even with suffering jet lag after thirty hours of economy class torture, I was short-listed to come back after the weekend for a round of presentations and further interviews. I made use of the time differences to create my presentation during the small hours of the night when I couldn't sleep.

Despite my herculean effort, I only managed to come second. The chief executive cited my lack of UK experience as the determining factor.

I flew back home exhausted. The company had promised to reimburse my flights, but it took six months of hassling them to get the money. I had also used up my leave for the rest of the year. The dream of having a stint working in the UK, living alongside Sara's English relatives, was our dream and with everything else going on we had not really asked the Lord about it. Now it had cost a lot of money, consumed my precious annual leave and been another source of emotional drain. I had spent myself down in the details instead of finding the mind of God.

We just didn't see the big picture. The end of the year came and so did a big surprise. I was home alone at midnight as Sara was out at a school Christmas celebration when the phone rang. It was the chief executive of the UK Crown Prosecution Service. In my half-dazed state, I immediately thought, 'They have caught up with me,' followed by, 'Hang on, I haven't done anything.'

Early into the conversation, Sara returned, and having forgotten her key, she banged on the window as I tried to sound alert and fully awake on the phone. It took a few minutes, but I soon realised that the chief executive was offering me a job; well, an interview at least. My curriculum vitae had been passed to him by the previous people who had interviewed me. Miraculously, the Crown Prosecution Service had had no joy in finding someone for the role in a country of around 60 million people.

God, the creator of the universe, had a big picture plan for us. And it was for our family to go to England.

Message to men (MTM)

Over the decades, Sara and I have seen families and marriages unravel when a man puts church ministry first.

They think it's God's will to be out endless nights and travelling about, spending little time at home. Well, it may be for a season, but it is certainly not God's will to neglect their primary responsibility and then to think foolishly that somehow it will be alright.

It's not alright and eventually we reap what we sow.[74] According to the Song of Solomon, marriage is like a garden. I take it from this that if you neglect your marriage by not weeding out the bad and fertilising the good it will become something you never intended. Marriage requires work and that means you need to be present and accounted for.

Listen carefully to this advice and don't become one of those men who has sat in my lounge with tears in his eyes because his family are off the rails, or they face seemingly irreconcilable differences in their marriage.

By wisdom a house [home] is built, and through understanding it is established …
Proverbs 24:3

Chapter Thirty-Seven
Fairy Tales and Marriage

Does everything need to be just right to stay in a marriage? If things are too hot to handle or have grown too cold for comfort should you, like Goldilocks, move on?

Many love affairs start off burning with passion. The desire to be with each other and to have each other seems almost unbearable. When you are apart, there is no one else that compares. When you are together, you claw at each other for attention and intimacy.

Sara and I used to be like that before we were married. As an engaged couple, who decided before God to hold back from having sex, we could not get enough of each other. The promise of more to come drove us almost insane with desire for each other. My life literally revolved on a Sara axis – where she filled most of my world.

Nowadays things are different. The hot passion has chilled and now the spicy cravings have smaller peaks and longer valleys. This leaves me facing the question: is our love better or worse than in those heady days?

We have also experienced times of cool. These happened when having young children, juggling work demands and church pressures squeezed every ounce of energy out of us, leaving us deeply exhausted. With persistent tiredness and tireless demands can come a tendency to let important things slip.

Subtly, you adopt survival mechanisms that shift your attention, using what time and energy you have to cope the best you can. This can mean staying longer at work or giving your all to the kids. Little by little you begin to radiate a signal that your spouse is no longer your number one priority and kick-start the ugly process of disconnecting from each other. Like the great continents, you slowly drift apart, a few millimetres at a time.

There is a school of thought on the internet that claims couples have a natural lifespan. These same websites have online surveys that you can take. Depending on the results, they may tell you that your relationship is not really worth it, or advise you to leave. The phrase 'seven-year itch' sums up what many think the life expectancy of love is. The irony of the saying is that it was made popular by one of the greatest sex symbols of the last century, Marilyn Monroe, in a 1955 film of the same name.[75] The itch implies a turbulent period of irritation and questioning about your marriage. It screams that it is time to consider your options, to look for something new that is 'just right' for you.

So why did the Father of all say that marriage is for life?[76] Why chain a man and woman to something that is impossible to sustain, let alone grow?

Let's go back to Goldilocks, who in the children's story moved from porridge, to chairs, to a bed before she finally found rest. There is a hint of menace in the fairy tale as (depending on your version of the story) it nearly cost her everything. To find out what was 'just right' she followed a typical pattern of taking what was not hers, breaking things and sleeping in another's bed.

Our quest as humans to find what is just right in our lives is almost always focused on the external. When things are too hot or too cold, it is usually someone else's fault. We judge love by a fickle barometer measured in emotions. If we don't feel the heat we once had for someone, we believe a storm is coming.

My advice at the end of this book is to quit your selfish quest for the 'just right' and throw away the barometer the world uses to measure love. Instead, introduce both science and faith to your relationship.

Science tells us that heat comes from vigorous motion. If you want more passion and a renewed longing for each other, then this requires deliberate, planned and prioritised action. And lots of it, starting with you. You must invest to save your marriage and, like all good investments, it will grow and return dividends given time.

We also need to be realistic. The hot stage of love is like the 'all you can eat' phase of the relationship. Eventually, you need to have a more balanced diet that is good for you both in the long-term. That is not to say we can't occasionally binge on wild passion, but like trying to live on takeaways, it is not sustainable in a healthy relationship.

The first principle to apply is that the onus to love rests with you. The force of active loving creates a reaction and like ice before the fire, eventually things will change.

Applying faith is not quite so easy as it is largely countercultural. The Bible tells us in the book of Ephesians 5 verses 25 and 33 that man is to love his wife 'as Christ loved the church' and that a woman is to 'respect her husband'. Let's look at that in reverse.

One of the common hot topics on the websites I have looked at is respect. They imply that if you no longer respect each other, it's over. But is respect for someone just something that is earned? On the face of it, that looks right but actually the Bible, which is our instruction manual on life, says otherwise. It tells us to actively respect others. Like love, respect is something we do; it's a choice we make.

That is quite different to what the world would tell us. What's more, the Bible puts the emphasis on the wife to respect the husband. When it boils down to it, every man wants to be esteemed by his loved one. Speaking well of him to others, bragging about him when in company, and listening to his advice is a huge factor in making him feel loved. For me, that is my true barometer of love.

Interestingly, the world portrays the romantic, the loving, the gentle and kind as feminine traits – but not according to the Bible. Men are instructed to love their wives selflessly like Christ modelled. The book on life also says that it is by kindness that God wins men to himself.[77]

What every woman wants to know is whether the man in her life is kind. This is the number one question residing in her mind, whether it is the first time they have met or after forty years of being together. Kindness and love are inseparable. Biblically, the responsibility is on the man to show love in ways that are focused on her, not on his wants and desires.

This seems almost impossible for most men – somehow, we are innately self-centred and egotistical. How can this ever be achieved; is it just the stuff of fairy tales? Well, it starts and ends with the focus not on her being 'just right', but on what I can do to be 'just right' for my beloved.

So, what about Sara and me – what would Goldilocks have to say about our marriage? Well, the early years were a whirlwind of events where life felt like a runaway train. One moment it seemed we went to sleep as newlyweds, the next we woke with three spritely ankle-biters at our feet.

Despite having waited almost seven years before the onslaught of family life, the hot phase didn't even last the honeymoon. Sex immediately became an issue. Given the opportunity, hindsight would beat me senseless telling me that I was unrealistic. My unfulfilled desires often left me feeling cold towards my wife. I gave her little latitude for the burdens she carried at the time and in my mind, it was hard to find enough times that were 'just right'.

With patience and persistence, usually from Sara rather than me, my small world has expanded into a much wider universe of appreciation for my wonderful wife. I have no wish to go back to the days of the hot passion and consuming desire as our love for each other is far deeper and better than ever before. Looking back to those days is embarrassing, as it was so often all about me.

Love is something you give away, not something you demand. It is a journey of discovery. For me, instead of being just a lover who always seemed to fall short, I have discovered a best friend and an amazingly wise confidante who is also full of surprises.

You may ask, what does a woman really want? I still don't know. But what I have realised is that they adore their partners trying to find out. My wife laps up my acts of kindness, she thrives on my affection, and every time I send out a resounding signal that announces she is my priority in life she melts with pleasure.

To get to this place has not been easy, nor has it been without cost. I have had to be teachable and perceptive. Sara has taught me how to be demonstrative when I did not know how. She has modelled for me what selfless love looks like.

My Sara is 'just right', even when she rejects my porridge, breaks my chairs, or is not sleeping in my bed. And if thirty-nine years of marriage is anything to go by, we will live happily ever after.

To me, Sara will always be 'just right'.

Message to men (MTM)

Our pastor once said, 'Our lives can be like living in a candy store. Endless choices and instant gratification, bringing about easy sin but it doesn't feed us.'

True love is not like a fairy tale, or candy floss that is all fluffy and light. While it experiences the full gambit of human emotions, it is also grounded in the practical and founded on hard work.

Unlike candy that gives a short-lived rush of energy but has no substance, love is more like a balanced diet. Each meal, like each day of marriage, may not be as memorable as a fairy tale chapter, but it builds a healthy body of love.

Love isn't perfect and it doesn't come easy, but it is worth fighting for.

Men, what you put into marriage is what you get out of it. This basic science tells us that we need to invest, to initiate, to ignite all that will help grow strong and lasting relationships.

You can do it, especially with the Lord at your side. The dream of living happily ever after is within your grasp. If you hold your wife tight in the arms of honour and respect, true love can be yours.

Your marriage will be like a magnificent garland of love that you wear.

A wife of noble character is her husband's crown …
Proverbs 12:4

Epilogue

Well, that's it – the early years on the journey we call marriage. This leg of the voyage ends with our family about to head to England in 1999.

At this point I am forty-one years old and feeling it. Work with Foreign Affairs and Trade has been immensely rewarding and successful, but has shifted to maintenance mode and become very political. As a pioneer, I am frustrated by this and suffer frequent migraines. My doctor tells me that I need to change jobs. After laughing off his comments that's exactly what I do. But it is not just me that needs a change. Both Sara and I are worn out by all the shenanigans in the church. Sara is about to hit the big Four-O and looking forward to a break from teaching. She is also ready for a new adventure and is excited about us living among her much-loved relatives in the UK.

Simon has just become a teenager and started high school. He is slightly moody as can be expected during this tumultuous time of life. Not surprisingly, he is searching for a faith where he is not just piggy-backing on his parents' beliefs. England for him becomes the perfect time of awakening where he meets his future wife and his faith grows to such an extent that he enters leadership at a young age.

Nat is still revelling in middle childhood and is absolutely delightful. He follows his brother, but certainly has a bubbly and friendly personality all of his own. This puts him in great stead in the UK making him extremely popular, especially among the girls. He is sporty, smart and into just about everything, including God.

Abi has only just turned seven and is still very much a little girl. She remains a paradox – a pretty little girl who loves dolls and girly things, but also very much at home playing rough and competing with the best of the boys (especially her brothers). Her outgoing personality becomes overshadowed by the move to the UK, which proves harder for her. She is at a different school to the boys for most of the time and finds breaking into the English cliques more difficult than they do. Nevertheless, she remains special to her dad and we enjoy many father-daughter dates together.

At this point in our lifelong adventure, Sara and I have enjoyed nineteen years of marriage. We have experienced much together, some of which is recorded in this book. There have been many new challenges and unexpected events, but there have also been some consistent things that have bonded us closer than can be expressed in words.

Our shared love for God as the source of all that is good has been the foundation on which we have built our marriage. Seeing each other as the number one priority above all else (other than the Lord) has shaped our family life and influenced many of the decisions we have made about careers and obligations. Much in life threatens those two principles through which we have filtered everything else, but we have stood together, unmoving in our commitment to them and to each other.

The only area where we have not been able to agree or find common ground has been over who steals the blankets at night. I know it's her. I know that I have married a blanket thief who comes in the dead of the night to steal away the covers and leave me cold and restless.

Of this I am sure, that she is guilty, and I intend to spend the rest of my natural life with her until I can prove it!

End Notes

1. See https://www.youthexchange.org.uk/ (accessed 24.1.19) for more information on Rotary Exchanges. Rotary has been organising year-long youth exchanges between countries for more than sixty years.
2. See 1 Corinthians 14.
3. See http://www.secretswekeep.com/how_we_fool_ourselves.htm (accessed 15.1.19).
4. This was a common term sometimes referred to as the normal distribution. It is used in education, psychology, economics and finance. For further information see https://www.investopedia.com/terms/b/bell-curve.asp (accessed 15.1.19).
5. C. McVie (1977), 'You Make Loving Fun' (Recorded by Fleetwood Mac on the album *Rumours* – USA: Warner Bros. Records).
6. Starring Stu Dennison in *Nice One Stu* on TVNZ, featuring in the late 1970s. http://www.nzonscreen.com/person/stu-dennison/biography (accessed 12.1.19).
7. See Judges 6.
8. 'New Life in the Spirit' seminars originated from the Catholic Church in the 1970s.
9. See 1 Corinthians 12:10.
10. See 1 Corinthians 12:8.
11. See Acts 1:5; Acts 2:38; Acts 8:16; Acts 10:47.
12. Used with permission by Island Escape Cruises. Taken from the Relaxing Journey Website describing the Bay of Island Cruise. http://www.relaxingjourneys.co.nz/cruises/ie/ieboi6.php (accessed 19.6.17).
13. For more information see Wikipedia on Carless Days in New Zealand http://en.wikipedia.org/wiki/Carless_days_in_New_Zealand (accessed 2.1.19).
14. Taken from a transcript of Senator Barack Obama's speech to supporters after the 5 February 2008 nominating contest during Super Tuesday in Chicago, Illinois. See: https://simple.wikiquote.org/wiki/Barack_Obama (accessed 15.1.19).
15. Used with permission by Holy Trinity Brompton. Gumbel, Nicky @ nickygumbel, Twitter: 7 November 2016. Also found in *Bible In One Year* (BIOY) by Nicky and Pippa Gumbel, see: https://www.bibleinoneyear.org (accessed 25.1.19).

16. Francis A. Schaeffer (1976, 2009), DVD: *How Should We Then Live: The Rise and Decline of Western Thought and Culture* (USA: Vision Video).

17. Attributed to Albert Einstein in *The Wall Street Journal*, 24 December 1997, article by Jim Holt, 'Science Resurrects God'. However, there seems to be no authoritative reference to that specific quote as being from the mouth of Einstein.

18. Used with permission by Penguin Books. Approximately eleven (11) words from *THE GO-BETWEEN* by L.P. Hartley (Hamish Hamilton 1953, London: Penguin Books 1958, 1997, 2000). Copyright 1953 by L.P. Hartley, Penguin Books 1997, 2000 editions. Copyright © Douglas Brooks-Davies 1997.

19. Used with permission by the Otago University. Philosophy of Science, 2017 http://www.otago.ac.nz/courses/papers/index. html?papercode=PHIL225 (accessed 15.1.19.)

20. Baruch Aba Shalev, *100 Years of Nobel Prizes* (New Delhi: Atlantic Publishers & Distributor, 2003), p. 57: an investigation into 100 years of Noble Prize winners (up to the year 2000) found that almost two-thirds of them had an affiliation with Christianity.

21. The biblical principle of giving 10 per cent of your income. See Genesis 14:19-20; Leviticus 27:30; Proverbs 3:9-10; Malachi 3:10-12; Matthew 23:23.

22. The reference to the 2014 study can be found at http://archive.stats. govt.nz/browse_for_stats/people_and_communities/Well-being/social-connectedness/social-networks/supportive-friends.aspx (accessed 15.1.19).

23. See https://www.theguardian.com/science/2015/jan/21/suicide-gender-men-women-mental-health-nick-clegg http://www.brake. org.uk/facts-resources/1593-driver-gender https://casapalmera. com/blog/the-facts-about-men-vs-women-and-alcoholism/ https://www.ncbi.nlm.nih.gov/pmc/articles/PMC 2235192/ https://assets.publishing.service.gov.uk/government/ uploads/system/uploads/attachment_data/file/759770/women-criminal-justice-system-2017..pdf https://www.canstar.co.nz/life-insurance/new-zealand-life-expectancy/ (accessed 23.1.19).

24. William Thomas Ellis, B*illy Sunday: The Man and His Message: With His Own Words Which Have Won Thousands for Christ* (Philadelphia, PA: John C. Winston Co, 1914).

25. Used with permission by Moody Publishers. A.W. Tozer, *Man: The Dwelling Place of God* (Harrisburg, PA: Christian Publications, Inc., 1966).

26. Taken from *What's So Amazing About Grace?* by Philip Yancey. Copyright © 1997 by Philip Yancey. Used by permission of Zondervan. www.zondervan.com.

27. Danzae Pace. Source unknown. Quoted on the Internet on sites such as https://www.goodreads.com/quotes/519858-stress-is-the-trash-of-modern-life-we-all-generate-it (accessed 16.1.19)

28. This quote is an anecdote about Rockefeller without evidence that he ever said this. It is found in the New World Encyclopedia and others sources http://www.newworldencyclopedia.org/entry/John_D._Rockefeller (accessed 2.1.19).

29. Although often attributed to Clint Murchison Jr., this saying, or variations of it, goes right back to Francis Bacon in 1625. Murchison quoted it as an adage he heard from his father. See https://quoteinvestigator.com/2016/02/05/muck/ (accessed 16.1.19).

30. Used with permission by The John Maxwell Co at http://www.johnmaxwell.com/ (accessed 16.1.19).

31. Used with permission by Liz Koh of Moneymax at www.moneymax.co.nz. Liz Koh (2010), *Grandma's Jars* – a blog on Askmumnow.com. http://www.askmumnow.com/money-matters/personal-financial-management/grandmas-jars/#sthash.QlHkVVj7.dpuf (accessed 16.1.19).

32. See https://en.wikiquote.org/wiki/Mark_Twain (accessed 16.1.19).

33. Read Adam's story in the opening chapters of Genesis.

34. See Luke 4.

35. Nora Ephron, *Heartburn* (Hachette Book Group, 1983). Deemed to fall under 'fair use' as established by the US Copyright office.

36. See Genesis 1:27; 1 John 4:8.

37. See 1 Corinthians 11.

38. See Hebrews 13:5.

39. Isaac Newton, 1675 see https://www.phrases.org.uk/meanings/268025.html (accessed 23.1.19).

40. Christian Johann Heinrich Heine (1848), Statement of 1848, as quoted in *The Cynic's Lexicon: A Dictionary of Amoral Advice*, ed. Jonathon Green (Abingdon: Routledge, 1984), p. 91.

41. Ibid.

42. Extract from *The House at Pooh Corner* by A.A. Milne. Text copyright ©

The Trustees of the Pooh Properties 1928. Published by Egmont UK Ltd. and used with permission regarding the UK and the Commonwealth. Used with permission for the rest of the world by Penguin Random House.

43. Extract from *The House at Pooh Corner* by A.A. Milne. Text copyright © The Trustees of the Pooh Properties 1928. Published by Egmont UK Ltd. and used with permission regarding the UK and the Commonwealth. Used with permission for the rest of the world by Penguin Random House.

44. Often misattributed to A.A. Milne and Winnie-the-Pooh.

45. W.L. Watkinson, 'The Invincible Strategy' in *The Supreme Conquest, and Other Sermons Preached in America* (Charleston, SC: BiblioLife, 2009). This quotation is often attributed to other sources including Eleanor Roosevelt.

46. The source cannot be verified as Winston Churchill. According to Wikiquote, this is misattributed to Winston Churchill as extensive research has failed to show that Churchill wrote or spoke this phrase. See https://en.wikiquote.org/wiki/Winston_Churchill (accessed 2.1.19). Some places have Norman MacEwen as the person with whom this quote originated, but this cannot be verified either.

47. Gary Chapman, *The Five Love Languages: How to Express Heartfelt Commitment to Your Mate* (Chicago, IL: Northfield Publishing, 1992).

48. Paraphrased from a quote by Kin Hubbard which first appeared in the *Saturday Review*, 18 March 1944, p. 19.

49. Often attributed to Bette Midler (*Herald Statesman*, section: Family Weekly 1980) or Marilyn Monroe (earliest attributions to Monroe were published decades after her death in 1962). See https://quoteinvestigator. com/2013/05/31/shoes-conquer/ (accessed 18.1.19)

50. Gary Chapman, *Everybody Wins: The Chapman Guide to Solving Conflicts Without Arguing* (Carol Stream, IL: Tyndale House Publishers, 2007).

51. Attributed to William Ashley (Billy) Sunday (1862-1935). Billy was an American evangelist and professional baseball player in the National League.

52. Used with permission by Maggie Gallagher who is an American writer and social commentator. Her website states that she is a thought leader on life, religious liberty and especially marriage – see http://maggiegallagher.com/ about/ (accessed 18.1.19).

53. From the Disney animated film, *The Lion King* (1994). Distributed by

Buena Vista Pictures.

54. Mary Shelley, *Frankenstein; or, The Modern Prometheus* (London: Lackington, Hughes, Harding, Mavor & Jones, 1818).

55. Jalaluddin Rumi , thirteenth-century Persian poet, jurist, Islamic scholar, theologian, and Sufi mystic. See https://www.thefamouspeople.com/profiles/rumi-20.php (accessed 18.1.19).

56. See Matthew 18:3.

57. James Oppenheim, *War and Laughter* (New York: The Century and Co., 1916).

58. For more information see: http://theconversation.com/americas-most-lethal-animal-45989 (accessed 18.1.19) and https://www.sciencealert.com/in-australia-bees-and-wasps-are-more-dangerous-than-spiders-and-snakes (accessed 18.1.19).

59. Used with permission by Leonard Ravenhill. Copyright © 1994 by Leonard Ravenhill, Lindale, Texas. http://www.ravenhill.org (accessed 18.1.19).

60. This is often attributed to Winston Churchill but there is little evidence for this. According to the Quote Investigator at: http://quoteinvestigator.com/2013/03/13/attitude-little-big/ (accessed 2.1.19) this quote is not found in *Churchill By Himself*, which is a comprehensive collection of Churchill quotations, ed. Richard Langworth (New York: PublicAffairs, 2011).

61. See https://simple.wikiquote.org/wiki/Charles_Spurgeon#cite_note-7 (accessed 18.1.19).

62. Mark Twain (1884), short story called *Taming the Bicycle* (CreateSpace Independent Publishing Platform, 2016).

63   PEANUTS © 1981 Peanuts Worldwide LLC. Dist. By ANDREWS MCMEEL SYNDICATION. Reprinted with permission. All rights reserved.

64. Attributed to Chris Hallman, BMX rider, photographer, and editor of *Tread Magazine*. See https://dcbikeblogger.wordpress.com/miscellaneous/quotes/ (accessed 18.1.19).

65. Often attributed to Albert Camus but researchers have been unable to locate this quotation in the writings of Albert Camus.

66. See https://en.wikiquote.org/wiki/Talk:Friendship (accessed 24.1.19).

67. Attributed to Aristotle who was an ancient Greek philosopher and scientist, 384-322 BC.

68. New Zealand term for gang members who wear identifying patches on their backs.
69. Anonymous; source unfound.
70. Used with permission by Albert Einstein Archives. Recalled by his Berlin student Esther Salaman, 1925, in Salaman, 'A Talk with Einstein', *The Listener* 54 (1955), pp. 370-371.
71. This quotation hasn't been found in any original work of A. A. Milne, but is often attributed to Eeyore.
72. New Zealand: a toy metal ring with beads. See also https://en.wikipedia.org/wiki/Chatter_ring (accessed 18.1.19).
73. *Topz* is a bi-monthly activity booklet aimed at seven to eleven year-olds to help them get to know the Bible. It is designed to make this fun by using cartoons, puzzles, word games etc. *Topz* is published by CWR in the UK. See http://www.cwr.org.uk/home (accessed 18.1.19).
74. See Galatians 6:7.
75. From the film, *The Seven Year Itch* starring Marilyn Monroe (1955). Distributed by 20th Century Fox.
76. See for example 1 Corinthians 7:10-11 and Romans 7:2.
77. See Romans 2:4.